WELCOME TO REAL

In today's world, eating healthy can be downright overwhelming. With countless names for artificial sugars, flavors, colors, chemicals, and other synthetic ingredients, it would appear that most of our grocery store shelves are filled with more "food-like products" than actual food. No wonder our stomachs are full, but our bodies are starving for nutrition.

Every new fad diet claims to be the true way to health while contradicting others that claim the same. If you're looking for a typical diet book, this is not the cookbook for you. In the following pages, we take food back to the basics: plants and animals. That's it. Inside, you'll find tried and true, flavor-packed recipes that are easy to make with ingredients you can feel good about eating.

We're on a mission to change as many lives as possible with the power of real, nutritious food. We hope you find joy in cooking each of our recipes and restored health as you learn to nourish your body with real food made simple.

Simply Yours,

Amanda & Nadia

First Printing, October 2023

ISBN: 979-8-218-29763-3 Published by Real Food Made Simple

Book Design by A.Brooke Creative

www.justrealfoodmadesimple.com

TABLE OF CONTENTS

KEY: ⊙ Quick & Easy   ⏱ Slow Cooker   🔥 Spicy   ❄ Freezes Well   ♨ Reheats Well

REFERENCE GUIDE

Throughout the book, we utilize various terms for settings, sizing, cookware, and food prep methods. You can use the information on these pages as a guide when following recipes.

CULINARY CUTS GUIDE:

We use a variety of terms to describe the preparation of vegetables, meats, herbs, etc. The visual below outlines the official culinary standard for each type of cut and how the terminology used within this book corresponds.

Note: For the purposes of this book, the term 'dice' generally refers to a medium dice, and 'fine dice' refers to a fine-small dice.

¼" Batonnet

⅛" Julienne

¾" Carré (Large Dice)

½" Parmentier (Medium Dice)

½" - ¾" Rough Chop

⅛"- ½" thick Rondelle (Slice)

¼" Macedoine (Small Dice)

<¹⁄₁₆" Mince

⅛"- ¼" Fine Chop

⅛" Brunoise (Fine Dice)

SUBSTITUTIONS:

If the recipe calls for...		You can substitute...
1 tablespoon **Fresh Herbs**	< >	1 teaspoon **Dried Herbs**
1 clove **Fresh Garlic**	< >	½ teaspoon **Garlic Powder**
⅛ - ¼ teaspoon **Extracts**	< >	1-2 drops high quality **Essential Oils**
1 can **Canned Beans**	< >	2 cups cooked/prepared **Dry Beans**

When in doubt, start with less and add more if necessary.

NUTRITIONAL FACTS:

You will notice that we don't have nutrition facts listed for any of the recipes. All of the foods in this cookbook are whole foods, and any amount can be eaten until satisfied. Our goal is to help you develop a well rounded diet with a variety of whole foods to ensure you get a variety of nutrients.

Stop counting your calories. Start counting your chemicals.

COOKWARE:

We only recommend using stainless steel, cast iron, and glass. While coated and non-stick pans are convenient, they are covered in chemicals which are released into the food and air when heated. These chemicals have been linked to reproductive issues, cancers, and other health problems.

Skillet Sizes
- **Small:** 7-8 inch
- **Medium:** 9-10 inch
- **Large:** 12-14 inch

Saucepan Sizes
- **Small:** 1 quart
- **Medium:** 1.5-2 quart

Stock Pot: 5-7 Quarts

Dutch Oven: 5-7 Quarts

Slow Cooker: 5-7 Quarts

RANGE SETTINGS:

Oven and cooktop temperatures are listed in each recipe. The list below gives numerical values that correspond with the average range. However, every oven and cooktop are different. If your range runs hotter or cooler than average, adjust accordingly.

Low: LO-2   **Medium-Low:** 3-4

Medium: 5-6   **Medium-High:** 7-8

High: 9-HI

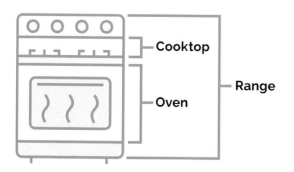

TEMPERATURE GUIDE:

Meat Type		Internal Temperatures
Steak/Beef	Rare	120°F - 125°F (49°C - 52°C)
	Medium-rare	130°F - 135°F (55°C - 57°C)
	Medium	140°F - 145°F (60°C - 63°C)
	Medium-well	150°F - 155°F (66°C - 68°C)
	Well done	160°F (71°C) and above
Poultry (Chicken or Turkey)		165°F - 175°F (74°C - 80°C)
Ground Meat		160°F (71°C)
Fish & Shellfish		145°F (63°C)
Casseroles & Baked Dishes		160°F (71°C)

Consumer Advisory: Consuming raw or undercooked meats, poultry, seafood, shellfish, or eggs may increase your risk of foodborne illness.

QUALITY FOOD STARTS WITH QUALITY INGREDIENTS

For thousands of years people have thrived eating plants and animals untouched from the way we find them in nature - aka real food. In other words:

"If it came from a plant, eat it; if it was made in a plant, don't."

When looking for whole foods, it's important to remember that in today's world not all foods are created equal. In the following pages are many of the guidelines we use to help choose the best available options no matter where you live.

DISCLAIMER!

Eat at your own risk! We are not medical professionals. The information recommended in this book is based on a compilation of advice from various medical professionals including medical doctors, nutritionists, natural health physicians, chiropractors, and many more who have spent years recommending this lifestyle to patients in their clinical practices and observing the successful results.

We are not liable for food borne illnesses or negative reactions resulting from the consumption of incorrectly cooked or poorly sourced ingredients. Please cook and eat at your own risk.

Don't take our word for it. Do your own research! *(PS: Google is no longer an unbiased resource.)*

Many of the mainstream platforms we are told to trust regarding food information are often incentivized to present data that may be misleading. We encourage you to look for information from non-biased sources such as independent studies (those not being funded by companies trying to make a profit from the sales of a product). Better sources can be found using alternative search engines. Sources that have been censored or aren't promoted in search results are also generally more truthful.

WHERE TO SHOP

BUY LOCAL:

Whenever possible, purchase your food from local, small farms. These farms generally have better quality meat and produce, and they are much more selective about what goes into and onto their products. Getting to know your local farmers and their methods provides confidence in the quality of products and treatment of animals, and ensures that small farms will continue to exist for future generations.

ONLINE:

Avoid big box chain stores. Whenever possible, purchase from companies that support small businesses and source from local farms.

For more information about products, organizations, and companies that we love and recommend, visit the resources page on justrealfoodmadesimple.com and follow us on social media @justrealfoodmadesimple.

Lemon Cucumber Mint Refresher (pg 48)

WATER

Whether it comes from city pipelines or a spring fed well, there can be contaminants in your water that you shouldn't be ingesting. Reverse Osmosis (R.O.) is a filtration process that uses pressure to force water through a semipermeable membrane, filtering out most contaminants. Utilizing a reverse osmosis water filtration system is the best way to ensure that the highest number of contaminants are removed. In short, ALL water needs to be filtered.

In-home water for drinking and cooking: There are many in-home R.O. systems you can purchase online. Many grocery stores also have these filtration systems available to refill reusable jugs for a small fee.

Bottled Water: Look for water that has been filtered by reverse osmosis and does not have added "vitamins", "nutrients", and flavors. Glass bottles are ideal, however if glass is not an option, look for bottles made from BPA free plastic.

DAIRY & DAIRY PRODUCTS

We Look For:

- Raw

- Grass-Fed and Grass-Finished

- Locally Sourced

- Pasture Raised

- Organic and Grass-Fed Grass-Finished (when raw is not available)

- Non-Homogenized and Low Temperature Pasteurized (when raw is not available)

- Imported: look for dairy from countries with more holistic regulations regarding product content and animal treatment

We Avoid:

- Heavily pasteurized and homogenized dairy products

- Added synthetic vitamins and minerals

- Coloring agents (like annatto in orange cheese based products)

- Pre-shredded cheeses with coatings

THE TRUTH ABOUT RAW DAIRY

Raw milk is an incredibly nutritious food that can provide many wonderful health benefits. Raw milk contains both lactose (a sugar) and lactase (an enzyme that breaks down that sugar). When milk is pasteurized, that enzyme is destroyed. For this reason, store bought milk causes digestive issues for many people.

Store bought milk typically contains synthetic vitamins and minerals which cannot be utilized by the body. However, raw milk is a great source of natural vitamins, minerals, enzymes, beneficial bacteria, and probiotics which can help improve digestion and boost immunity.

Disclaimer: There are many stances found online regarding the safety of raw dairy. It's important to do your own research using reliable sources and to make an informed decision for yourself. We recommend realmilk.com and the Weston A. Price Foundation as reliable sources of information about raw milk.

MEATS

We Look For:

- Organic. No Hormones Added. No Antibiotics.
- Grass-Fed, Grass-Finished Beef
- Pasture-Raised Chicken
- Wild-Caught Fish: Cod, Salmon, Mahi Mahi, Flounder
- Wild or Pasture-Raised Turkey
- Pasture-Raised Lamb
- Wild Game: Bison, Buffalo, Deer, Elk

We Avoid:

- Pork: Pigs eat nearly anything (including garbage and dead animals) and are often fed plastics along with low quality feed. Because they lack sweat glands, they have no efficient way of detoxing from the garbage that they eat, which means it's absorbed into the meat that you eat. Pork includes items like ham, bacon, sausage, salami, pepperoni, etc.
- Farm raised fish (like tilapia) are fed grains and other unnatural food including artificial coloring agents to give the appearance of fresher fish.
- Turkey bacon, chicken sausage, and other similar meats are commonly thought of as healthier options, but are in fact more heavily processed.
- Grain-Fed Animals: Grain-fed animals are fed corn, soy, and other GMO grains.

FRUITS & VEGGIES

We Look For:

- Organic. Non-GMO.
- In Season
- Locally Grown/Native

You can eat an unlimited amount of vegetables each day.

Your vegetable intake should be at least 3-4 times more than your fruit intake.

We Avoid:

- High starch, low nutrient items (like white potatoes and corn)
- High sugar fruits (eaten in excess)

OILS & FATS

It's important to choose oils based on two factors: content and smoke point.

CONTENT:

We Look For:

- Animal Fats: Grass-Fed Butter, Tallow, Ghee
- Organic, Unrefined, Expeller Pressed Oils: Coconut, Avocado, Olive
- Glass Containers

SMOKE POINT:

It's important to note the difference between cooking oils and cold oils. Cooking oils have high smoke points and can be used for medium and high heat cooking. Cold oils have low smoke points and are best used unheated in sauces and dressings.

Cooking Oils:

- Medium-High: Avocado, Coconut, Tallow, Ghee
- Low-Medium: Grass-Fed Butter

Cold Oils:

- Olive

All of these options are great sources of healthy fats and contain only mild flavors that complement dishes well.

We Avoid:

- Refined Oils
- Vegetable Oil and Peanut Oil
- Genetically Modified: Soy, corn, canola, and cotton are the most common genetically engineered crops and their oils are extremely high in unhealthy polyunsaturated fats.
- Seed Oils: Sunflower, Cottonseed, Safflower, Sesame Seed, Canola, Grapeseed, Soybean, etc.

ESSENTIAL OILS

Put simply, essential oils are highly concentrated plant extracts. Most people only think of essential oils being used in a diffuser or topically, but they can also be used in the kitchen. Essential oils are commonly used in cooking as substitutions for fresh herbs, spices, and extracts like vanilla, peppermint, lemon, cinnamon, etc.

However, it's important to note that not all essential oils are created equal and not all oils are safe for ingestion. Most store-bought essential oils are diluted with fillers and are extracted using chemical solvents.

We Look For:

- Companies that avoid harmful practices
- Companies whose values and ethics align with ours
- Oils that do not contain any fillers or chemicals
- Oils that are known to be safe for ingesting

Disclaimer: There are many varied opinions found online about the safety and efficacy of essential oils. It's important to do your own research using reliable sources and to make an informed decision for yourself.

NUTS & SEEDS

Nuts and seeds are a great source of healthy fats, protein, minerals, and more.

We Look For:

- Organic. Non-GMO.
- Raw or Dry Roasted

We Avoid:

- Peanuts & Peanut Butter: Although peanuts are technically a legume, they are most generally categorized as a nut. Peanuts are the only "nut" we don't recommend eating. Even organic and non-GMO peanuts and peanut butters can have an incredibly high mold content that can lead to inflammation and an increase in problematic symptoms.
- Nuts roasted in oils we avoid
- Nuts with added sugars, flavors, and/or colors

HERBS & SPICES

Always be sure to check the ingredients list on spices. Although you would assume spices are just spices, many brands contain ingredients that you wouldn't want to ingest.

We Look For:

- Organic. Non-GMO.

We Avoid:

- Anti-Caking Agents
- Starches (Corn, Potato, Rice, etc.)
- Added Sugars
- Natural Flavors
- Artificial Colors

GRAINS

Grains are not what they used to be. Here are a few of the reasons we don't recommend eating them on a regular basis.

- They are currently the most genetically modified crop in the world.

- They are grown in depleted soil, fed chemical fertilizers, and sprayed with toxic herbicides and pesticides.

- They are stripped of the few nutrients they do have for shipping and preserving purposes.

- Grains only retain their nutrients for a small amount of time after being milled, therefore, store bought flours are almost always rancid.

- Grains turn to sugar in our bodies and can cause inflammation, which inhibits healing.

Hundreds of years ago, grains were grown in healthier soil, prepared properly, and eaten by people doing hard physical labor all day long. They were necessary to keep people alive during the cold winter months when fresh foods were scarce.

If you are going to eat grains, we recommend doing the following:

- Purchasing whole grains that are Organic/Non-GMO

- Grinding your own grains to ensure you are using only freshly ground flour

- Eating them occasionally and only in limited quantities

LEGUMES & PSEUDO-GRAINS

A legume is a term for plants with pods that have edible seeds inside them. Legumes include beans, chickpeas, lentils, peas, etc. Beans are legumes, but not all legumes are beans.

Pseudo-grains are seeds of grasses that cook like grains. Pseudo-grains contain protein and fiber, are lower on the glycemic index, provide a wide variety of vitamins and minerals, and are easier to digest than grains.

We Look For:

- Organic. Non-GMO.
- Dried (best)
- Canned (BPA-free cans)

We Avoid:

- BPA cans
- Pre-seasoned

PROCESSED FOODS

As a general rule, we recommend limiting processed food items as much as possible. There are many companies that produce lightly processed items without the addition of synthetic or unhealthy ingredients (aka garbage). A good rule of thumb is to never buy a product if it contains ingredients that are heavily processed or that you can't pronounce.

We Look For:

- Whole food ingredients
- Organic. Non-GMO.
- A limited number of ingredients

We Avoid:

- Ingredients that we avoid in their whole form (corn, rice, wheat, etc.)
- Artificial Colors, Flavors, & Sweeteners
- Natural Flavors
- Synthetic Preservatives: Sodium Benzoate, Sulfites, Polyphosphates, Sorbates, Nitrites, etc.
- High Fructose Anything
- Any sweetener not on the approved list (see below)

SWEETENERS

We recommend limiting sweeteners to special occasions.

We Look For:

- Organic. Non-GMO.
- Local Raw Honey (Do Not Heat)
- Pure Maple Syrup
- Unrefined Coconut Sugar
- Dates or Date Syrup
- Bananas

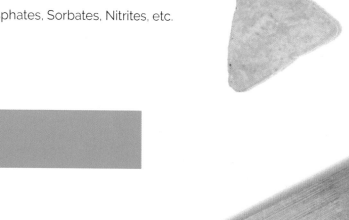

We Avoid:

- Artificial Sweeteners (see pg 16)
- High Fructose Anything
- Sugar Alcohols (Erythritol, xylitol, maltitol, etc.)
- Stevia: while stevia is technically a whole food, it is a major endocrine system disrupter and has been linked to infertility.

FOOD TERMINOLOGY

There are many terms being thrown around haphazardly on the market today. It is crucial to understand what these terms mean in order to make the best, most informed decisions regarding the foods you buy.

100% Certified Organic: Food or products produced without the aid of chemical or synthetic fertilizers, pesticides, herbicides, insecticides, fungicides, antibiotics, or artificial growth hormones.

❶ Artificial Colors: Artificial colors are found in foods everywhere. Awareness of their adverse health effects is becoming more prevalent. Independent research studies have shown that artificial colors contribute to behavioral problems, reduction in cognitive functions, and more.

The most common artificial colors are Red #40, Red #3, Blue #1, Blue #2, Yellow #5, Yellow #6, and Green #3.

❶ Artificial Flavors: Man-made compounds synthesized in a lab that are used to enhance and standardize the flavor of packaged food and beverages.

As with "natural flavors," there are thousands of GRAS (generally recognized as safe) chemicals that are allowed by the FDA to fall under this label without disclosing their use or inclusion in the final product.

Artificial flavors have been shown to impact our food cravings, increase toxic load, and can lead to nutritional deficiencies and other health problems.

❶ Artificial Sweeteners: Synthetic, lab produced, chemical sweeteners. Products containing artificial sweeteners are labeled as a "healthier" choice due to the lack of natural fats and sugars. However, independent research studies have abundantly shown that these chemicals are directly linked to a number of health problems such as cancer, diabetes, weight gain, mood changes, pain, disturbed vision, migraines, nausea, memory loss, nerve damage, organ damage, and seizures.

The most common artificial sweeteners are Equal (aspartame and acesulfame potassium), Nutrasweet (aspartame), Splenda (sucralose), Sweet N Low (saccharin), and Sweet One (acesulfame potassium).

❶ Bioengineered Food: Recently recognized by the federal government, the term "bioengineered" (abbreviated "BE") is the new term for genetically modified organisms (❶ GMOs). The USDA defines bioengineered foods as "those that contain detectable genetic material that has been modified through lab techniques and cannot be created through conventional breeding or found in nature."

Since many products are created with new GMO techniques that are currently untestable, manufacturers may not be required to use BE labeling. Lacking a commercially available test, the modified genetic material is "technically undetectable." To make matters worse, a product made with multiple ingredients may be exempt from requiring a BE label due to the order in which the ingredients are listed.

With all the technical limitations, exemptions, and loopholes in the BE labeling laws, many products made with BE ingredients will not require a disclosure.

Cage-Free: Refers to poultry or other animals that were not kept in cages. They may still have been confined to a building with limited space and without access to fresh air or sunlight.

❶ Fat-Free: Products that contain no more than 0.5 grams of fat per serving. These items can and often do contain refined oils, artificial flavors, added sugars, and other unhealthy ingredients. Also labeled as, "low fat (no more than 3 grams of fat per serving)," "non-fat," or "zero fat."

Free-Range or "Free-roaming": Refers to poultry or other animals that were "given access to the outside," although this can be interpreted numerous ways. Even though their habitat may or may not really be free, this poultry can legally be labeled "free-range."

Gluten Free: Products that do not contain gluten, a protein found in wheat, barley, and rye. However, these products can still contain grains that have gone through processing to remove the gluten molecule. These processes damage the integrity of grain, making it even less healthy and possibly harmful to your health.

Items marked with this symbol should be avoided in your regular diet.

Grass-Fed: A term that can be placed on any animal that was fed grass at some point during its life. Animals not also labeled as grass-finished were likely fed primarily grains, which they would not normally eat.

Grass-Finished: Animals that spend their entire lives eating grass, plants, and shrubs on pastures, with the exception of milk consumed prior to weaning.

Made with Organic Ingredients: 70% of the product must be organic. The other 30% is unregulated.

Natural Flavors: Oils, resins, and other extractions derived from plant or animal sources that are used to enhance and standardize the flavor of packaged food and beverages.

Natural flavors can be sourced from anything natural, including bugs, genetically modified plants, and beaver anal glands! (Yes, really...) The term "natural" refers to the original extraction source, but does not account for any chemicals added afterward. There are thousands of GRAS (generally recognized as safe) chemicals allowed by the FDA to fall under this label without disclosing their use in a product. In many cases, "natural flavors" may contain more chemicals than artificial versions.

Non-GMO: Food and products made without ingredients that were derived from genetically engineered organisms. Meat, poultry, dairy, and eggs with a "non-GMO verified" label are from animals that were not fed a diet containing genetically engineered crops.

Organic: 95% of the product must be organic. The other 5% is unregulated. Organic is a vague term. Dirt is technically organic.

Paleo: Refers to the hunter-gatherers of the historical past and their diet of lean meats, fish, vegetables, fruits, nuts, and seeds and strictly limiting foods such as dairy products, legumes, grains, potatoes, and refined sugar.

Pasture-Raised: Poultry or other animals that are not kept in small pens but instead are free to roam and graze on pastures for most of the day.

Sugar Free: Products that contain less than 0.5 grams of sugar per serving. These items can and often do still contain artificial sweeteners. Also labeled as, "free of sugar," "no sugar," or "zero sugar."

Vegan: A diet that excludes all food derived from animals, including honey.

Vegetarian: A diet that excludes all meat or fish and sometimes other animal products.

Wild Caught: Fish that live in their natural habitats that are caught by fishermen.

REAL FOOD PANTRY

This list includes all of the delicious whole food ingredients we used to create the recipes in this cookbook. Many of our favorites are in this list, but there are many other wonderful options to explore! We recommend regularly varying the foods you consume to maximize your intake of unique nutrients.

Veggies
baby spinach
beets
bell peppers
broccoli
broccoli sprouts
Brussels sprouts
butternut squash
cabbage
carrot
cauliflower
cauliflower rice
celery
cucumbers
eggplant
green beans
green onion
green peas
jalapeños
kale (various kinds)
lettuce
mixed greens
mushrooms
onions (various kinds)
parsnips
poblanos
sweet potatoes
tomatoes
(various kinds)
zucchini

Fruit
apples
avocados
bananas
lemons
limes
mangos
Medjool dates
peaches
strawberries

Freezer
avocado chunks
banana
brussels sprouts
cauliflower
green peas
mango chunks
strawberries

Herbs & Spices
basil, fresh or dried
black pepper
cayenne pepper
chili powder
cilantro, fresh
or dried
curry powder
dill, fresh or dried
fennel seed
garlic cloves
garlic powder
ginger, fresh
ground cinnamon
ground coriander
ground cumin
ground ginger
ground nutmeg
ground turmeric
marjoram, dried
mint leaves
mustard powder
onion powder
oregano, dried
parsley, fresh
or dried
red pepper flakes
rosemary, fresh
or dried
sage, dried
sea salt
smoked paprika
thyme, fresh or dried

Legumes & Pseudo-Grains
black beans
cannellini beans
chickpeas/hummus
dark red kidney beans
lentils (various kinds)
pinto beans
quinoa
white beans

Proteins
chicken, breasts
chicken, whole
chuck roast
cod filets
collagen powder
eggs
ground beef
protein powder:
chocolate, vanilla,
or unflavored
salmon filets
scallops
smoked salmon
steaks
turkey

Broths
beef broth
beef bone broth
chicken broth
chicken bone broth

Dairy
raw milk
raw or grass-fed
butter and ghee
raw or grass-fed
cheeses: parmesan,
feta, etc.

Oils
avocado oil
coconut oil
olive oil
tallow

Canned Goods
artichoke hearts
coconut cream,
unsweetened
diced tomatoes
olives
pasta sauce
pepperoncinis (no
dyes or preservatives)
pumpkin puree
salsa
strawberry jam
or preserves
sundried tomatoes
tomato juice
tomato paste

Sweeteners
maple syrup
raw honey

Vinegars
apple cider vinegar
balsamic vinegar
distilled white vinegar
red wine vinegar
white wine vinegar

Condiments
avocado mayonnaise
balsamic vinaigrette
barbeque sauce
buffalo sauce
coco aminos
dijon mustard
hot sauce
ketchup

Beverages
almond milk,
unsweetened
coconut milk,
unsweetened
coffee, organic
reverse osmosis
filtered water

Dry Goods
almond flour
baking powder,
aluminum free
cacao nibs
cassava flour
cocoa powder,
unsweetened
coconut flour
coconut shreds,
unsweetened
flaxseed meal
matcha powder

Nuts & Seeds
almonds
almond butter
cashews
cashew butter
chia seeds
hemp hearts
mixed nut butter
pecans
pumpkin seeds
sesame seeds
sunflower seeds
walnuts

Misc
lemon juice
lime juice
peppermint extract
vanilla extract

BREAKFAST

APPLE CINNAMON QUINOA "OATMEAL"

Servings:	Prep time:	Cook time:	Wait time:
2-3	5 minutes	25 minutes	3 minutes

What You'll Need:

- 1 cup quinoa
- 2 cups water
- 1 medium apple
- 3-4 pitted Medjool dates
- 2-3 teaspoons ground cinnamon
- ⅛ teaspoon sea salt, or to taste
- ¼ teaspoon vanilla extract, optional
- 2 tablespoons butter
- ½ tablespoon raw honey or maple syrup, optional

What To Do:

1. Finely dice apple and dates.
2. Thoroughly rinse quinoa under cool water and drain using a fine mesh strainer.
3. Add quinoa and water to a medium saucepan. Stir to combine.
4. Bring to a rolling boil over high heat.
5. Add apple, dates, and cinnamon. Stir to combine.
6. Reduce heat to low, cover, and simmer for 10 minutes.
7. Stir quinoa, re-cover, and continue to cook for 5 minutes.
8. Remove the saucepan from the heat and allow the quinoa to rest, covered, for 3 minutes.
9. Add salt, vanilla, and butter. Fluff quinoa with a fork to combine.
10. Serve topped with honey or maple syrup and an extra sprinkle of cinnamon.

EGG VEGGIE CASSEROLE

Servings:	**Prep time:**	**Cook time:**	**Wait time:**
5-6	15 minutes	25-35 minutes	None

What You'll Need:

- 1 small onion
- 8 oz mushrooms, any variety
- 1 medium zucchini
- 1 small bell pepper
- 3 cloves garlic
- 10 eggs
- ¼-½ cup grated cheese, any variety
- 2-3 teaspoons Mediterranean Spice Mix (pg 86) or seasonings of choice
- ½ teaspoon sea salt, or to taste
- ½ teaspoon black pepper, or to taste
- ¼ teaspoon red pepper flakes, optional
- 1 tablespoon cooking oil

What To Do:

1. Preheat the oven to 350°F.
2. Dice onions, mushrooms, zucchini, and bell pepper. Mince garlic.
3. Heat a large skillet over medium heat. When the skillet is hot, add oil.
4. Add mushrooms, veggies, and garlic. Cook for 7-10 minutes or until veggies are soft.
5. Remove the skillet from the heat.
6. In a large bowl, beat eggs and seasonings together until fully combined.
7. Spread cooked veggies evenly into a medium-large, oiled baking dish. Pour egg mixture over veggies.
8. Bake for 15-20 minutes or until eggs are mostly cooked through.
9. Remove from the oven and top with cheese.
10. Bake for 5 additional minutes or until cheese is melted and eggs are cooked through.
11. Add additional salt and pepper to taste.
12. Optional: Top with red pepper flakes.

CAST IRON BREAKFAST FRITTATA

Servings:	Prep time:	Cook time:	Wait time:
4-6	20 minutes	30 minutes	5 minutes

What You'll Need:

- 1 ½ cups veggies*
- 1 cup cooked chicken, beef, or turkey**
- 2 tightly packed cups baby spinach
- 1 cup grated cheese, any variety
- 10 eggs
- 1 tablespoon garlic powder
- 2 teaspoons onion powder
- 1 teaspoon sea salt
- ½ teaspoon black pepper
- ½ teaspoon red pepper flakes, optional
- 2 tablespoons cooking oil

Optional Toppings:
fresh salsa (pg 90), diced avocado, cheese, hot sauce

What To Do:

1. Preheat the oven to 375°F.
2. Dice veggies and meat into bite-sized pieces.
3. Heat a deep or large cast iron skillet over medium heat. When the skillet is hot, add oil.
4. Add diced veggies and cook for 5-7 minutes or until veggies just begin to soften.
5. Add spinach and cook for 1-2 minutes.
6. Add meat, stir to combine, and turn off heat.
7. In a large bowl, beat eggs and spices together until fully combined.
8. Pour egg mixture into the skillet over the meat and veggie mixture. Top with cheese, and immediately place into the oven.
9. Bake for 15-22 minutes or until eggs are cooked through.
10. Remove from the oven and allow frittata to rest for 5 minutes before serving.

*Our favorites are onions, mushrooms, tomatoes, bell pepper, zucchini, and sweet potato, but you can use any combination

**If using pre-seasoned meat, reduce salt by 50%. If your meat is particularly fatty, drain some of the fat out before adding to the mixture.

HEARTY STUFFED OMELETS

Servings:	Prep time:	Cook time:	Wait time:
1 omelet, 1-2 servings	10 minutes	10-12 minutes	None

What You'll Need:

- 1 loosely packed cup baby spinach
- ¼ cup mushrooms, any variety
- 3-4 cherry tomatoes
- 1 tablespoon green onions
- 3 eggs
- 1 tablespoon milk (raw or almond), optional
- 1 tablespoon feta cheese
- ½ teaspoon dried parsley
- ½ teaspoon garlic powder
- ¼ teaspoon smoked paprika
- ⅛ teaspoon sea salt, or to taste
- ⅛ teaspoon black pepper, or to taste
- 1 tablespoon cooking oil
- 1 tablespoon butter

Optional Toppings:
fresh salsa (pg 90),
diced avocado, hot sauce

What To Do:

1. Dice spinach, mushrooms, tomatoes, and green onion.
2. Heat a medium skillet over medium heat. When the skillet is hot, add butter, onion, and mushrooms. Cook, stirring frequently, for 5-7 minutes or until onion is tender.
3. Stir in spinach and cook for 1-2 minutes or until wilted. Pour the contents of the skillet into a small bowl and set aside.
4. In a medium bowl, beat eggs, milk, herbs, and spices together until fully combined.
5. Reheat the skillet over medium heat and add oil. Pour in egg mixture, stirring quickly for 10-15 seconds or until eggs are somewhat set, but still slightly liquid. Stop stirring, reduce heat to low, cover, and cook for 1-2 minutes. **Note:** Omelet will continue to cook after folding.
6. Remove the lid. Sprinkle cooked veggie mixture, tomato, and cheese onto half of the omelet.
7. Slide spatula fully under one edge of the omelet and slowly work around the edge of the skillet, loosening the omelet. If the mixture is too soft to separate cleanly, increase heat to medium-low and cook 20-30 seconds longer.
8. With the spatula beneath the side opposite the veggie mixture, carefully fold the omelet in half.
9. Gently slide the finished omelet onto a plate and serve immediately.

TIP: We recommend using an 8-10 inch skillet with rounded sloping sides. This makes folding an omelet easier!

SWEET POTATO BREAKFAST HASH

Servings:	**Prep time:**	**Cook time:**	**Wait time:**
4-6	15-20 minutes	30-40 minutes	None

What You'll Need:

Baked Veggies:

- 2 medium sweet potatoes
- 2 medium bell peppers
- 1 medium onion
- 1 teaspoon sea salt
- ½ teaspoon garlic powder
- ½ teaspoon smoked paprika
- ¼ teaspoon black pepper
- 1 ½ tablespoons cooking oil

Eggs:

- 5 eggs
- 1 tablespoon dried parsley
- ½ teaspoon chili powder
- ¼ teaspoon sea salt
- 1 tablespoon cooking oil

Optional Toppings:

fresh salsa (pg 90), diced avocado, cheese, hot sauce

What To Do:

1. Preheat the oven to 400°F.

2. Dice veggies into bite-sized pieces.

3. In a large bowl, combine all baked veggie ingredients. Spread mixture evenly across an oiled sheet pan.

4. Bake for 25-30 minutes or until sweet potatoes are fork tender and just starting to crisp.

5. In a medium bowl, beat eggs, parsley, chili powder, and salt together until fully combined.

6. When the veggies are almost cooked, heat a large skillet over medium heat. When the skillet is hot, add oil.

7. Pour egg mixture into the skillet. Stir constantly for 1-2 minutes or until eggs are almost completely cooked.

8. Remove the skillet from the heat and stir occasionally for 2-3 minutes. Eggs will continue to cook once removed from the heat.

9. When veggies are fully cooked, stir them into the skillet to combine with the eggs.

GROUND BEEF SAUSAGE PATTIES

Servings:
2-4

Prep time:
8 minutes

Cook time:
10 minutes

Wait time:
None

What You'll Need:

- 1 pound ground beef
- 2 teaspoons sea salt, or to taste
- 2 teaspoons garlic powder
- ½ teaspoon smoked paprika
- ½ teaspoon black pepper
- ½ teaspoon ground cumin
- ½ teaspoon fennel seed
- ¼ teaspoon dried thyme
- ¼ teaspoon dried sage
- ¼ teaspoon red pepper flakes
- 1 tablespoon cooking oil, optional

What To Do:

1. Mix all ingredients except the oil together in a large bowl.
2. Gently shape the mixture into patties that are approximately 2 inches wide and ½ inch thick.
3. Press a small divot into the center of each patty with your thumb to allow for more even cooking.
4. Heat a large skillet over medium-high heat. When the skillet is hot, add oil.
5. Place the sausage patties into the skillet and cook for 1-2 minutes or until browned.
6. Flip the patties in the same order you placed them.
7. Cook for 1-2 additional minutes or until patties are cooked through.
8. Transfer immediately to a serving plate to ensure that the patties do not overcook.

CHOCOLATE BANANA FLAXSEED PANCAKES

Servings:	Prep time:	Cook time:	Wait time:
2-3	10 minutes	10-15 minutes	None

What You'll Need:

- ½ cup flaxseed meal
- 1-2 tablespoons unsweetened cocoa powder
- ¾ teaspoon aluminum free baking powder
- ½ teaspoon ground cinnamon
- ⅛ teaspoon sea salt
- 1 large ripe banana*
- 2 eggs
- ¼ cup milk
- 1 teaspoon vanilla extract
- 1 tablespoon cooking oil

Optional Toppings:
butter, fresh fruit, nut butter, maple syrup, raw honey

What To Do:

1. Mix all dry ingredients together in a large bowl.
2. Add banana, eggs, milk, and vanilla. Use a fork to mash banana and beat eggs, slowly combining with dry ingredients until the texture is consistent throughout.
3. Heat a large skillet over medium heat. When the skillet is hot, add oil.
4. Spoon about 2 tablespoons of batter onto the skillet for each pancake, and gently spread the mixture for more even cooking.
5. Cook each pancake for 2-3 minutes or until bubbles appear and begin to pop and the sides begin to firm.
6. Carefully flip and cook for 2-3 additional minutes, or until each pancake is firm.
7. Transfer to a plate, top with optional toppings, and serve immediately.

TIP: If making a larger batch, heat the oven to the lowest baking temperature and store cooked pancakes on a sheet pan inside until ready to eat!

*TIP: Riper bananas have a sweeter taste. If you have an under-ripened banana, preheat the oven to 350°F. Place a banana (peel on) on a sheet pan, and bake for 7 minutes or until the peel is mostly brown. Remove from the oven and allow to cool 2-3 minutes before peeling. The banana will be soft and perfectly sweet!

EGG & AVO SWEET POTATO "TOAST"

Servings:	Prep time:	Cook time:	Wait time:
3-4	15-20 minutes	35-40 minutes	3-4 minutes

What You'll Need:

Sweet Potato Toast:

- 2 medium sweet potatoes
- 1 teaspoon cooking oil
- ¼ teaspoon garlic powder
- ⅛ teaspoon sea salt
- ⅛ teaspoon smoked paprika

Eggs:

- 4 eggs
- 1 tablespoon fresh cilantro
- ¼ teaspoon garlic powder
- ¼ teaspoon sea salt
- ⅛ teaspoon chili powder
- 1 teaspoon cooking oil

Topping:

- 2 ripe avocados
- ¼ teaspoon garlic powder
- ¼ teaspoon sea salt
- Fresh salsa (pg 90), optional

What To Do:

1. Preheat the oven to 400°F.

2. Peel sweet potatoes and cut lengthwise into ¼ inch slices. Lightly oil both sides of each slice, sprinkle with garlic powder, smoked paprika, and salt, and place onto a sheet pan.

3. Bake for 35-40 minutes or until cooked through and slightly toasted, flipping every 10-12 minutes.*

4. While sweet potato slices are baking, peel and pit avocados. Mash avocados, garlic, and salt together with a fork until mixture is mostly smooth.

5. Remove "toast" from the oven and allow to cool 3-4 minutes.

6. Finely dice cilantro.

7. Heat a skillet over medium heat. When the skillet is hot, add oil.

8. Cook eggs to your preference (scrambled, fried, sunny side up, etc.). Immediately remove from the heat and top with cilantro, garlic powder, salt, and chili powder.

9. Transfer "toast" pieces to a plate or serving tray and top with mashed avocado, eggs, and salsa.

10. Extra "toast" can be stored in a sealed container in the refrigerator for up to 1 week.

*This recipe is meant to be eaten with a fork. If you want the "toast" to be easy to pick up, bake until extra crispy, flipping every 5 minutes.

MAIN DISHES

SCALLOP FRIED QUINOA

Servings:	Prep time:	Cook time:	Wait time:
3-4	12 minutes	30-37 minutes	None

What You'll Need:

- ½ pound small scallops*
- 3 eggs
- 1 cup quinoa
- ½ cup coco(nut) aminos
- 1 ¾ cup water
- ¼ cup green onion
- ½ cup green peas
- 1 large carrot
- ½ medium zucchini, optional
- 2 cloves garlic
- ½ teaspoon sea salt
- ½ teaspoon black pepper
- ½ teaspoon ground cumin
- ¼ teaspoon curry powder, optional
- 4 tablespoons cooking oil

Optional toppings:
sesame seeds, fresh grated ginger, red pepper flakes, green onion

What To Do:

1. Rinse scallops thoroughly with cool water, then pat dry with paper towels. Allow to air dry as you prepare quinoa and veggies.

2. Thoroughly rinse quinoa under cool water and drain using a fine mesh strainer.

3. Add quinoa and water to a medium saucepan. Stir to combine.

4. Bring to a rolling boil over high heat. Then, reduce heat to low, cover, and simmer for 10 minutes.

5. While quinoa is cooking, mince garlic and dice green onion. Dice or julienne carrots and zucchini.

6. Add ¼ cup coco(nut) aminos to the quinoa and stir to combine. Re-cover and cook for 5 additional minutes. Remove the saucepan from the heat and allow the quinoa to rest, covered, for 3 minutes. Remove the lid and fluff quinoa with a fork.

7. Heat a large skillet over medium heat. When the skillet is hot, add 2 tablespoons of oil.

8. Add carrots and zucchini. Cook, stirring frequently, for 5-7 minutes or until veggies are almost tender.

9. Add green peas, garlic, and green onion. Stir to combine. Cook for 2-3 additional minutes or until veggies are fork tender.

10. Transfer cooked mixture to a large mixing bowl and set aside.

11. Add 1 tablespoon of oil to the skillet. Add bay scallops in a single layer and cook for 2 minutes. Increase heat to medium-high, flip scallops, and cook for 1 additional minute. Immediately transfer scallops into the bowl with the veggie mixture.

12. Optional: Add 2 tablespoons of oil to the skillet. Add the quinoa and continue to cook over medium-high, stirring frequently, for 5-7 minutes or until quinoa becomes slightly crispy.

13. Add quinoa, seasonings, and remaining ¼ cup of coco(nut) aminos to the mixing bowl. Stir to combine with veggies and scallops.

14. Heat a separate small skillet over medium heat. When the skillet is hot, add 1 tablespoon of oil. Add eggs and stir constantly for 3-4 minutes or until eggs are completely cooked. Immediately transfer eggs to the bowl and stir to combine.

*Look for scallops that are small (30/40 per pound) like bay scallops or Farrow Island scallops.

GROUND BEEF STUFFED PEPPERS

Servings:
4-8

Prep time:
20 minutes

Cook time:
30 minutes

Wait time:
None

What You'll Need:

- 1 pound ground beef
- 4 large bell peppers
- 1 small onion
- 1 can (15 oz) black beans, drained
- 1 can (15 oz) diced tomatoes, drained
- ¼ cup feta cheese or other cheese variety
- 3 cloves garlic
- 2 teaspoons ground cumin
- 1 ½ teaspoons chili powder
- ½ teaspoon smoked paprika
- 1 teaspoon sea salt, or to taste
- ½ teaspoon black pepper, or to taste
- 1 tablespoon cooking oil

What To Do:

1. Preheat the oven to 400°F.
2. Cut bell peppers in half and remove the stems, seeds, and membranes.
3. Place the bell pepper halves cut side up on an oiled sheet pan. Sprinkle ½ teaspoon salt and pepper on top.
4. Bake for 15 minutes or until slightly softened.
5. Dice onion and mince garlic.
6. Heat a large skillet over medium heat. When the skillet is hot, add oil.
7. Add onions and cook for 4-5 minutes or until they start to become translucent.
8. Add ground beef and garlic. Continue to cook, stirring frequently, for 5-7 minutes or until meat is broken up and thoroughly cooked.
9. Add chili powder, cumin, smoked paprika, and remaining salt.
10. Stir to combine.
11. Add beans and tomatoes and cook for 5 minutes.
12. Spoon mixture into softened peppers and top with cheese.
13. Bake for 5 additional minutes.

MEDITERRANEAN MIXED BOWLS

Servings:	Prep time:	Cook time:	Wait time:
3-4	15 minutes	20 minutes	3 minutes

What You'll Need:

- 1 cup quinoa
- 16 oz broth (pg 18) or water
- 1-2 tablespoons fresh cilantro
- 1-2 tablespoons Mediterranean Spice Mix (pg 86) or seasoning blend of choice
- 1 tablespoon butter

Optional Toppings:
(We recommend at least four!)

- 1 tightly packed cup baby spinach
- ¼ cup hummus
- ⅓ cup smoked salmon or other cooked meat
- 10 olives, quartered
- ¼ cup broccoli sprouts
- 2 tablespoons pickled onion*
- 2 tablespoons pickled cucumber*
- 2 tablespoons feta cheese
- ½ an avocado

What To Do:

1. Thoroughly rinse quinoa under cool water and drain using a fine mesh strainer.

2. Add quinoa and broth to a medium saucepan. Stir to combine.

3. Bring to a rolling boil over high heat. Then, reduce heat to low, cover, and simmer for 10 minutes.

4. While quinoa is cooking, gather and prepare your toppings.

5. Stir quinoa, re-cover, and continue to cook for 5 minutes.

6. Remove the saucepan from the heat and allow the quinoa to rest, covered, for 3 minutes.

7. Add cilantro, seasonings and butter to the quinoa. Fluff quinoa with a fork to combine.

8. Layer bowls with quinoa and your preferred toppings, saving the meat for last.

9. Serve as is, or toss together with a simple vinaigrette.

*TIP: For easy pickled veggies, finely dice then place into a jar. Cover with white vinegar and add ½ teaspoon of sea salt for each cup of diced veggies. Shake to combine and allow to soak for at least 30 minutes before serving.

13

HEARTY BLACK BEAN SWEET POTATO BAKE

Servings:	Prep time:	Cook time:	Wait time:
4-6	20 minutes	20 minutes	3 minutes

What You'll Need:

Quinoa Black Bean Base:

- 1 cup quinoa
- 16 oz broth (pg 18) or water
- 1 can (15 oz) black beans, drained
- 3 teaspoons chili powder

Sweet Potato Filling:

- 2 large sweet potatoes
- 1 teaspoon sea salt
- ¼ cup butter
- 2 cloves garlic

Mango Salsa Topping:

- 2 Roma tomatoes
- ½ cucumber
- 1 large mango
- 1 tablespoon lime juice
- 1 tablespoon fresh cilantro
- 1 teaspoon sea salt

What To Do:

1. Peel and chop sweet potatoes into 2-inch cubes. Place the cubes into a stock pot, add 1 teaspoon salt, and cover with water.

2. Bring to a rolling boil over high heat. Then, reduce heat to medium-low and simmer for 15-20 minutes or until cubes are fork tender.

3. Base: While sweet potatoes are boiling, thoroughly rinse quinoa under cool water and drain using a fine mesh strainer.

4. Add quinoa and broth to a medium saucepan. Stir to combine.

5. Bring to a rolling boil over high heat. Then, reduce heat to low, cover, and simmer for 10 minutes.

6. Stir quinoa, re-cover, and continue to cook for 5 minutes.

7. Remove the saucepan from the heat and allow the quinoa to rest, covered, for 3 minutes.

8. Add black beans and chili powder. Fluff quinoa with a fork to combine.

9. Filling: Mince garlic. Drain cooked potatoes, add butter and garlic, and mash until smooth.

10. Topping: Peel, pit, and dice mango. Dice tomatoes and cucumber. Mix mango, tomato, and cucumber together with lime juice, cilantro, and remaining salt.

11. Layer a 9x13 baking dish with quinoa black bean mix on bottom, followed by sweet potatoes, then top with salsa mixture. This dish can be served warm or chilled.

CHEESY TACO PIE

Servings:	Prep time:	Cook time:	Wait time:
4-6	15 minutes	35-40 minutes	None

What You'll Need:

- 1 pound ground beef
- 6 eggs
- ½ -1 cup grated cheese
- 2 cloves garlic
- ½ teaspoon sea salt, or to taste
- 1 teaspoon black pepper, or to taste
- 2-3 tablespoons taco seasoning

Optional Toppings:
3 diced avocados, 1 large diced tomato, fresh salsa (pg 90), green onions

What To Do:

1. Preheat the oven to 350°F.

2. Heat a large cast iron skillet over medium-high heat. Add ground beef and cook, stirring frequently, for 5 minutes or until meat is broken up and mostly cooked.

3. Stir in taco seasoning and spread beef evenly across the skillet or a medium-large glass baking dish.

4. Mince garlic. In a large bowl, mix together eggs, garlic, salt, and pepper. Pour this mixture over the ground beef and sprinkle cheese on top.

5. Bake for 30 minutes or until eggs are cooked through and cheese is browned.

6. Top with avocado, salsa, and green onions.

TIP: This dish can be prepped up to 12 hours in advance. Cook beef, pour egg mixture on top, cover, and refrigerate until ready to bake. Just before baking, sprinkle cheese on top. Bake for 10 additional minutes to accommodate for the cold baking dish and ingredients.

BONUS RECIPE: **Taco Seasoning**

- 5 teaspoons smoked paprika
- 1 ½ teaspoons garlic powder
- 1 ½ teaspoons ground cumin
- 1 ½ teaspoons sea salt
- 1 teaspoon onion powder
- 1 teaspoon chili powder
- 1 teaspoon dried oregano

ITALIAN BAKED MEATBALLS

Servings:	Prep time:	Cook time:	Wait time:
2-3	10 minutes	18-22 minutes	2 minutes

What You'll Need:

• 1 pound ground beef

• ½ small onion

• 3 cloves garlic

• 1 teaspoon sea salt, or to taste

• 1 tablespoon Italian seasoning

Optional Toppings:
pasta sauce, shredded
cheese, red pepper flakes

What To Do:

1. Preheat the oven to 400°F.

2. Finely dice onion. Mince garlic.

3. Add all ingredients to a bowl and mix until thoroughly combined.

4. Using your hands, form mixture into small meatballs roughly 1 ½ inches in diameter and place onto a walled sheet pan.

5. Bake for 18-22 minutes or until meatballs are cooked through.

6. Allow meatballs to rest for 2 minutes before serving with optional toppings.

Notes:

• This dish pairs well with fresh baked spaghetti squash.

BONUS RECIPE: **Italian Seasoning**

•2 tablespoons dried basil

•2 tablespoons dried oregano

•2 tablespoons dried parsley

•1 tablespoon dried rosemary

•1 tablespoon dried thyme

•1 teaspoon garlic powder

•1 teaspoon dried marjoram, optional

HERB BASTED STEAK

Servings:	Prep time:	Cook time:	Wait time:
2	5 minutes	10-15 minutes 6-10 minutes	5 minutes

What You'll Need:

- 2 steaks (6-10 oz each)*
- 3 tablespoons butter
- 2 cloves garlic
- 1 teaspoon sea salt, or to taste
- 2 sprigs fresh or ½ teaspoon dried rosemary
- 2 sprigs fresh or ½ teaspoon dried thyme
- 1 tablespoon cooking oil

What To Do:

1. Mince garlic and set aside.
2. Wash fresh herbs or measure dried herbs and set aside. If using fresh herbs, do not separate them from the stem.
3. Use paper towels to pat the steaks dry and evenly salt both sides.
4. Heat a large cast iron skillet over medium-high heat. Once the skillet is hot, add oil.
5. Place steaks into the skillet and sear each side for 2 minutes.
6. Once both sides have been seared, reduce the heat to medium. Add butter, garlic, and herbs to the skillet distributed evenly beside the steaks.
7. Flip the steaks every 30 seconds, allowing both sides to soak up the butter, garlic, and herbs for 1-2 minutes or until the steaks are almost to your desired doneness.

8. Then, tip the skillet to the side, and use a spoon to baste the steaks with the herb butter. Do this for about 30 seconds, then flip the steaks and repeat.
9. Continue to cook and baste, flipping the steaks every 30 seconds, until the steaks reach your desired doneness.** Then, immediately remove from the skillet.
10. Transfer to plates and serve immediately, or transfer to a cutting board and allow to rest, covered, at least 5 minutes before slicing against the grain.
11. Pour the remaining warm herb butter from the skillet over the steaks once plated.

*Ribeye, fillet, strip, and t-bone steaks that are approximately 1.5 inches thick are ideal for this recipe. We advise against using flank or skirt steaks.

**We recommend using a meat thermometer along with a doneness chart to determine when to remove your steaks from the heat.

SWEET POTATO SHEPHERD'S PIE

Servings:	Prep time:	Cook time:	Wait time:
6	40 minutes	45-50 minutes	5 minutes

What You'll Need:

Sweet Potato Topping:

- 3 medium sweet potatoes
- 4 tablespoons butter
- ½ teaspoon garlic powder
- ½ teaspoon chili powder
- ½ teaspoon sea salt, or to taste
- ½ teaspoon dried oregano
- ½ teaspoon dried parsley
- ½ teaspoon ground cumin

Pie Filling:

- 1 pound ground beef
- 2 medium carrots
- 1 small yellow onion
- 1 medium bell pepper
- 1 cup green peas
- ½ cup beef broth
- 2 tablespoons tomato paste
- 2 tablespoons cassava flour, optional
- 2 teaspoons garlic powder
- 1 teaspoon sea salt, or to taste
- 1 teaspoon black pepper
- ½ teaspoon smoked paprika
- ½ teaspoon chili powder
- ¼ teaspoon dried oregano
- ¼ teaspoon dried rosemary or thyme
- 1 tablespoon cooking oil

What To Do:

1. Peel and chop sweet potatoes into 2-inch cubes. Place the cubes into a stock pot and cover with water.
2. Bring to a rolling boil over high heat. Then, reduce heat to medium-low and simmer for 20-25 minutes or until cubes are fork tender.
3. Drain water and add butter, herbs, and spices. Stir and mash with a fork or potato masher until potatoes reach a mostly smooth consistency.
4. While sweet potatoes are boiling, dice carrots, onion, and bell pepper.
5. Heat a medium skillet over medium-high heat. When the skillet is hot, add oil.
6. Add diced veggies, cover, and cook for 8 minutes, stirring frequently.
7. Add ground beef and cook, stirring frequently, for 5-7 minutes or until veggies are soft and meat is broken up and thoroughly cooked.
8. Reduce heat to medium-low. Add peas and pie filling herbs and spices. Stir to combine.
9. Preheat the oven to 375°F.
10. In a high-powered blender or food processor, blend ½ cup of meat and veggie mixture together with tomato paste and broth.
11. Pour blended mixture into the skillet and add cassava flour. Stir to combine. Allow to simmer for 2-3 minutes, stirring frequently as the mixture thickens.
12. Transfer meat and veggie mixture to a 9x13 baking dish and spread evenly.
13. Spread sweet potato mixture evenly across the top, making sure the meat mixture is completely covered.
14. Bake for 10 minutes. Then, broil for 2-3 minutes or until potatoes start to lightly brown.
15. Remove from the oven and allow to rest for 5-7 minutes before serving.

BLACKENED HERB SALMON

Servings:
2

Prep time:
10 minutes

Cook time:
8-12 minutes

Wait time:
10 minutes

What You'll Need:

- 2 salmon filets (4-6 oz each)
- 1-2 tablespoons cooking oil
- ¼ teaspoon sea salt
- ½ teaspoon garlic powder
- ½ teaspoon smoked paprika
- ¼ teaspoon dried thyme
- ¼ teaspoon onion powder
- ¼ teaspoon black pepper
- ¼ teaspoon dried basil
- ¼ teaspoon dried oregano
- ⅛ teaspoon cayenne powder, optional

What To Do:

1. For even roasting, remove salmon filets from the refrigerator 10 minutes prior to cooking.
2. Preheat the oven to 400°F.
3. Add oil, herbs, and spices to a small bowl. Stir until thoroughly combined.
4. Use paper towels to pat the salmon dry and place skin down on a sheet pan.
5. Rub seasoning mixture into the top of the salmon.
6. Bake for 8-12 minutes or until salmon is cooked through.

ROSEMARY LEMON WHOLE CHICKEN

Servings:	Prep time:	Cook time:	Wait time:
2-6	35 minutes	≈ 1 hour 30 minutes	40 minutes

What You'll Need:

• 1 whole chicken (3-5 pounds), fully thawed

• 1 large onion

• 1 large sweet potato

• 3 parsnips or carrots

• 1 lemon

• 5 cloves garlic or 1 tablespoon garlic powder

• 2 tablespoons fresh rosemary

• 1 tablespoon sea salt

• 1 tablespoon black pepper

• ⅓ cup butter

• 2 tablespoons cooking oil

What To Do:

1. For even roasting, remove chicken from the refrigerator 30 minutes prior to cooking.

2. Preheat the oven to 475°F.

3. In a small saucepan, melt butter. Mince garlic, finely dice rosemary, and zest lemon. Stir these along with salt and pepper into melted butter. Remove from the heat and allow to cool.

4. Peel and dice sweet potatoes, onions, and parsnips or carrots into bite-sized pieces. Add diced veggies and oil to a large Dutch oven. Stir until veggies are thoroughly coated.

5. Remove giblets from chicken (if applicable).

6. Use paper towels to pat the chicken dry and remove excess moisture from the skin.

7. Place the chicken on top of the diced veggies.

8. Pour cooled butter mixture over chicken, making sure to coat as much of the skin as possible. If butter has slightly hardened, use a spatula or your hands to spread the mixture.

9. Cut lemon in half. Squeeze lemon juice over chicken and veggies, being careful to catch and remove seeds.

10. Place lemon rinds inside the chicken.

11. Bake chicken uncovered for 15 minutes.

12. Reduce heat to 350°F and bake 20 minutes per pound*, or until internal temperature reaches 165°F. Only cover the Dutch oven if chicken begins to burn.

13. Allow chicken to rest for at least 10 minutes before carving.

14. After carving, remove roasted veggies from the Dutch oven. Spoon remaining juices over the chicken to add extra flavor.

*For example: A 3 pound chicken should be baked for 60 minutes after reducing the heat to 350°F.

JUICY HOMESTYLE MEATLOAF

Servings:	Prep time:	Cook time:	Wait time:
5-6	20 minutes	50-55 minutes	5 minutes

What You'll Need:

Meatloaf:

- 2 pounds ground beef
- ½ medium onion
- 1 small bell pepper
- 2 eggs
- ¼ cup milk (raw or almond)
- ½ cup ketchup (pg 94)
- 1 tablespoon coco(nut) aminos
- 3 cloves garlic
- 2 tablespoons fresh parsley (pg 7)
- 1 teaspoon Italian seasoning (pg 34)
- 1 teaspoon sea salt, or to taste
- ½ teaspoon smoked paprika
- ½ teaspoon mustard powder
- ½ teaspoon black pepper

Sauce:

- ¼ cup ketchup (pg 94)
- ¼ cup barbeque sauce (pg 95)

What To Do:

1. Preheat the oven to 375°F.
2. Finely dice or mince onion, bell pepper, garlic, and parsley.
3. In a large bowl, beat eggs, milk, ketchup, coco(nut) aminos, and seasonings together until fully combined. Add all other meatloaf ingredients and mix to combine.
4. Gently transfer mixture to an oiled loaf pan. Smooth mixture evenly into the pan by pressing lightly. Make sure not to pack meat too tightly or it will become dense.
5. Mix sauce ingredients together. Pour half of the mixture over the meatloaf and gently spread to cover the meat.
6. Bake for 35 minutes, then remove from the oven and top with remaining sauce mixture.
7. Bake for 10-15 additional minutes or until meat is cooked through.
8. Remove from the oven and allow to rest for 5 minutes before serving.

CRISPY SPATCHCOCK CHICKEN

Servings:	Prep time:	Cook time:	Wait time:
2-6	15-20 minutes	45-55 minutes	35 minutes

What You'll Need:

- 1 whole chicken (3-5 pounds), fully thawed
- 6 tablespoons softened butter or ghee
- 1 tablespoon Italian seasoning (pg 34)
- 2 tablespoons garlic powder
- 2 teaspoons smoked paprika
- 2 teaspoons sea salt
- 1 teaspoon black pepper

What To Do:

1. For even roasting, remove chicken from the refrigerator 30 minutes prior to cooking. Place the butter or ghee on the counter at this time as well to soften.

2. Preheat the oven to 400°F.

3. Use paper towels to pat the chicken dry. Place breast-side down on a large cutting board.

4. Using sharp kitchen scissors*, cut along one side of the spine, separating it from the ribs. To avoid removing excess meat, cut as close to the spine as possible. Cut halfway along one side of the spine, then repeat on the other side of the spine. Continue cutting both sides until the spine is removed. If you have difficulty, rotate the bird and cut from the opposite side.

5. Flip the chicken over. Push down in the center using the heel of your palm to break the breast bone and allow chicken to lay flat.

6. Place the chicken breast side up on a sheet pan.

7. In a bowl, combine butter or ghee and all seasonings.

8. Using your fingers, separate chicken skin from chicken.** Place most of the butter mixture under chicken skin and press down. Rub the remaining mixture on the outside of the chicken.

9. Bake for 45-55 minutes or until chicken is cooked through.***

10. Remove from the oven and allow to rest for 5 minutes before carving and serving.

Important Notes:

*You will need sharp kitchen scissors to be able to easily cut through thicker bones around the spine.

**Initially getting under the skin may require a bit of patience. Once you "break" beneath it, the rest is easy!

**We highly recommend using gloves as you will be getting your entire hand covered in raw chicken, oil, and seasoning.

***Some smoke may occur while baking. We recommend having a range hood fan on.

MISSISSIPPI POT ROAST

Servings:
3-4

Prep time:
5-10 minutes

Cook time:
8 hours

Wait time:
None

What You'll Need:

- 2-3 pounds chuck roast*
- 8-10 whole or ⅓-½ cup sliced pepperoncini peppers**, with juice***
- 3-5 cloves garlic
- 1-2 tablespoons onion powder
- 2 tablespoons dried parsley
- 1 teaspoon sea salt
- 1 teaspoon black pepper
- 2 tablespoons butter or ghee

What To Do:

1. For a milder spice level, remove seeds from pepperoncini peppers.
2. Place all ingredients into a slow cooker.
3. Set the slow cooker to low and cook for 8 hours.
4. Dice finished roast into small pieces or pull apart into shreds using forks.
5. Serve with juices poured on top.

*You can use a frozen or defrosted chuck roast for this recipe. If defrosted, double the amount of butter/ghee.

**Look for pepperoncini peppers with no dyes or preservatives. If you prefer less spice, we recommend using sliced peppers. If you prefer more spice, you can add additional peppers!

***Leave just enough juice to cover the peppers remaining in the jar.

CILANTRO LIME CHICKEN

Servings:	Prep time:	Cook time:	Wait time:
3-4	15 minutes	15-30 minutes	30+ minutes

What You'll Need:

- 1 pound chicken breasts
- ½ cup fresh cilantro
- 2 tablespoons lime juice
- 2 cloves garlic
- 1 teaspoon ground cumin
- 1 teaspoon sea salt
- 1 teaspoon black pepper
- ½ teaspoon smoked paprika
- 2 tablespoons cooking oil

What To Do:

1. Mix or blend all ingredients except chicken together. If the mixture seems too thick, add additional oil. **Note:** If you are not using a blender, mince garlic and finely chop cilantro before mixing.

2. Place the chicken and marinade mixture into a bag or sealable container.

3. Allow chicken to marinate in the refrigerator for at least 30 minutes.

Baking Method:

1. Preheat the oven to 375°F.

2. Pour the chicken and marinade mixture into a glass baking dish.

3. Bake for 20-30 minutes or until chicken is cooked through.

Cooktop Method:

1. Heat a cast iron skillet over medium heat. When the skillet is hot, add chicken breasts and marinade mixture.

2. Cook for 5-8 minutes on each side or until chicken is cooked through.

GARLIC PARMESAN CHICKEN TENDERS

Servings:
2-4

Prep time:
18 minutes

Cook time:
15-20 minutes

Wait time:
10 minutes

What You'll Need:

- 1 pound chicken breasts
- 1 egg
- ¼ cup almond flour
- ⅓ cup cassava flour
- ½ cup finely grated parmesan cheese
- ½-¾ teaspoon garlic powder
- ½-¾ teaspoon smoked paprika
- ½ tablespoon dried parsley
- ½ teaspoon sea salt, or to taste
- ½ teaspoon black pepper
- ½ teaspoon chili powder

What To Do:

1. For even baking, remove chicken from the refrigerator 10 minutes prior to cooking.

2. Preheat the oven to 375°F.

3. Cut breasts into slices roughly ½ inch thick and 3-4 inches long.

4. Use paper towels to pat the chicken dry.

5. Combine both flours, cheese, herbs, and spices in a large bowl.

6. In a separate bowl, beat the egg.

7. Dip each chicken breast into the egg, then immediately toss in the flour mixture until thoroughly coated.

8. Place onto a lightly oiled sheet pan. Make sure pieces are at least one inch apart for best cooking results.

9. Bake for 15 minutes or until chicken is cooked through.

LEMON GARLIC BAKED COD

Servings:	Prep time:	Cook time:	Wait time:
2	10 minutes	10-15 minutes	None

What You'll Need:

- ½ pound cod filets
- 1 lemon
- 1 teaspoon fresh parsley (pg 7)
- ½ teaspoon sea salt, or to taste
- ¼-½ teaspoon garlic powder
- ¼ teaspoon black pepper
- ¼ teaspoon smoked paprika, optional
- 1 ½ tablespoons butter

What To Do:

1. Preheat the oven to 400°F.
2. Finely dice parsley and set aside.
3. Place cod filets in a glass baking dish. Lightly press thicker parts of the cod to thin out for more even cooking.
4. Sprinkle filets with spices except parsley and top with slices of butter.
5. Cut lemon in half. Squeeze juice from one lemon half over the filets.
6. Slice remaining lemon half into thin circular slices and remove seeds. Place 1-2 slices of lemon onto each fillet.
7. Bake for 10-15 minutes or until cod is cooked through. **TIP:** An easy test is to press on a thicker part of the cod with the back of a fork. If cod easily flakes apart and is no longer translucent in the center, it's done!
8. Once plated, use a spoon to drizzle remaining lemon juice and butter from the dish over the cod and top with parsley.

LOADED EGGPLANT PARMESAN

Servings:
2-4

Prep time:
30 minutes

Cook time:
35-40 minutes

Wait time:
None

What You'll Need:

Eggplant:

- 1 medium eggplant
- 1 egg
- ⅓ cup almond flour
- ⅓ cup cassava flour
- ⅓ teaspoon sea salt
- ⅓ teaspoon dried basil
- ⅓ teaspoon dried oregano
- ¼ teaspoon black pepper
- ¼ teaspoon smoked paprika
- ¼ teaspoon onion powder

Topping:

- 8 oz mushrooms, any variety
- 4-5 cloves garlic
- 4 loosely packed cups baby spinach
- ½ cup pasta sauce
- ¼ cup sundried tomatoes
- ½ cup grated parmesan cheese
- 1 tablespoon cooking oil

What To Do:

1. Preheat the oven to 400°F.
2. Slice eggplant into ¼-inch thick rounds.
3. Combine both flours, herbs, and spices in a medium bowl or plate.
4. In a separate bowl, beat the egg.
5. Place each eggplant slice into egg and flip to completely coat. Place the slice onto the flour, press down and lightly twist while holding onto the edges of the slice. Flip the slice and repeat the press and twist process. Place the coated slices onto an oiled sheet pan. Make sure pieces are at least one inch apart for best cooking results.
6. Bake for 40 minutes or until eggplant is tender and starting to crisp.
7. While eggplant is baking, dice mushrooms, finely dice garlic, and roughly chop spinach.
8. Heat a large skillet over medium-high heat. When the skillet is hot, add 1 tablespoon of oil.
9. Add diced mushrooms and cook, stirring occasionally, for 5-7 minutes or until they begin to turn golden brown. Transfer mushrooms to a medium bowl and set aside.
10. Add garlic and spinach to the skillet. Reduce heat to medium and cook, stirring frequently, for 3-4 minutes or until spinach is fully wilted.
11. Reduce heat to medium-low, stir in pasta sauce, sun dried tomatoes, and mushrooms, and simmer 2-3 minutes.
12. Reduce heat to low and stir occasionally until eggplant is ready.
13. When eggplant is done, spoon 1-2 tablespoons of pasta sauce mixture onto each eggplant slice. Top each slice with 1-2 tablespoons of parmesan cheese.
14. Bake for 5-10 additional minutes or until cheese is melted.

ZUCCHINI LASAGNA BOWLS

Servings:	Prep time:	Cook time:	Wait time:
4-6	45 minutes	50 minutes	40+ minutes

What You'll Need:

- 3 medium-large zucchini
- 1 pound ground beef
- 8 oz sliced mushrooms, optional
- 1 medium onion
- 1 tablespoon oil
- 2 ½ teaspoon sea salt
- 2 teaspoons garlic powder
- 2 tablespoons Italian seasoning (pg 34)
- 24 oz pasta sauce
- 2-3 tablespoons cassava flour
- 1 cup grated parmesan cheese
- 1-2 cups grated cheese

What To Do:

1. Slice zucchini into ⅛-¼ inch rounds. Using a mandolin or vegetable slicer makes this much easier.

2. Spread a large absorbent kitchen towel across the counter. Cover with a layer of paper towels. This will prevent lint from sticking to your zucchini. Place the zucchini slices across the paper towels in a single layer. Sprinkle 2 teaspoons of salt evenly across the slices. Top with a layer of paper towels and another kitchen towel.

3. Place a flat object such as a large cutting board or sheet pan on top. Add weight evenly across the top. Heavy items like cast iron skillets and canned goods work great.

4. Allow the zucchini to sweat for at least 30 minutes. The longer you wait, the more water will be absorbed by the towels. For best results, the zucchini should be as dry as possible.

5. While the zucchini sweats, dice the onion.

6. Heat a large skillet over medium-high heat. When the skillet is hot, add 1 tablespoon of oil.

7. Add onion and cook for 3-5 minutes.

8. Add ground beef and mushrooms. Cook, stirring frequently, for 5 minutes or until meat is broken up and mostly cooked.

9. Add garlic, Italian seasoning, and remaining ½ teaspoon of salt and cook for 2-3 additional minutes. Remove the skillet from the heat and set aside.

10. Combine both cheeses together in a bowl.

11. Remove weights from zucchini and uncover.

12. Preheat the oven to 375°F.

13. Layer your lasagna ingredients in a deep medium-large baking dish in the following order: zucchini slices, a light sprinkle of cassava flour, pasta sauce, ground beef mixture, and cheese. Repeat this layering until all your ingredients are used up. Keep in mind you will want your final layer to be a larger amount of cheese.

14. Bake for 30 minutes or until the cheese is nicely browned.

15. Remove from the oven and allow to cool for 10 minutes before serving.

TIP: This dish stays together better after overnight refrigeration, so leftovers are recommended.

DRINKS & SHAKES

EVERYDAY GREEN SHAKE

Servings:	Prep time:	Cook time:	Wait time:
2-3	7 minutes	None	None

What You'll Need:

- 3 cups water or milk
- 1 moderately packed cup baby spinach
- 1 moderately packed cup kale
- 4 frozen Brussels sprouts
- 1 medium carrot
- 1 frozen banana or ½ cup frozen strawberries
- 2 tablespoons nut butter (pg 87)
- ½ teaspoon ground cinnamon
- 2 scoops vanilla protein powder or collagen powder
- ½ avocado, optional

What To Do:

1. Add all ingredients to a high-powered blender. Blend on high until mixture is smooth.

CHOCOLATE MINT VEGGIE SHAKE

Servings:	Prep time:	Cook time:	Wait time:
1-2	10 minutes	None	None

What You'll Need:

- 1 frozen banana
- 1 small parsnip
- 1 loosely packed cup baby spinach
- 1 loosely packed cup kale
- 2 cups milk
- 3 tablespoons chocolate protein powder or 2 tablespoons unsweetened cocoa powder
- 2 tablespoons nut butter
- ¼ teaspoon vanilla extract
- ⅛ teaspoon peppermint extract

What To Do:

1. Roughly chop parsnip.
2. Add all ingredients to a high-powered blender. Blend on high until mixture is smooth.

LEMON CUCUMBER MINT REFRESHER

Servings:	Prep time:	Cook time:	Wait time:
6-8	5 minutes	None	1 hour

What You'll Need:

- 1 gallon water
- 1 large cucumber
- 2 lemons
- 10-15 fresh mint leaves
- ¼-½ teaspoon sea salt
- 2 tablespoons apple cider vinegar, optional
- Ice cubes, optional

What To Do:

1. Slice cucumber into ½ inch circular slices.
2. Place lemons on the counter. Firmly press down on each lemon with the palm of your hand and roll back and forth to gently break apart the inner membranes. This allows for more juice and flavor.
3. Cut both lemons into slices, and remove as many seeds as possible.
4. Place mint leaves into one hand and gently smack them with the other. This warms the mint slightly and starts to extract oils before adding it to the drink.
5. Add all ingredients to a pitcher and stir to combine.
6. Refrigerate at least 1 hour and stir prior to pouring.

CREAMY COLD BREW

Servings:	Prep time:
1	10 minutes
Cook time:	**Wait time:**
None	12 hours

What You'll Need:

- 1 ½ cups cold water
- ⅓ cup freshly coarse-ground organic coffee beans, any roast
- ½ cup milk
- 2-3 teaspoons maple syrup
- Ice cubes (regular or milk)

What To Do:

1. Spoon ground coffee into a glass jar, container, or French press that is 12 oz or larger.

2. Gently pour in water and carefully stir until all grounds are wet.

3. Cover the container and allow it to sit on the counter for at least 12-18 hours.

4. Optional: Pour extra milk into an ice cube tray and freeze while coffee is steeping.

5. Taste periodically to determine strength and flavor. When the cold brew reaches your desired flavor and strength, strain into a glass using a fine mesh strainer.

6. Add maple syrup and stir to thoroughly combine.

7. Add ice, leaving a couple inches of space at the top of the cup.

8. Froth milk in a separate glass using a frothing whisk or blend in a blender for 10-15 seconds.

9. Pour frothed milk over coffee.

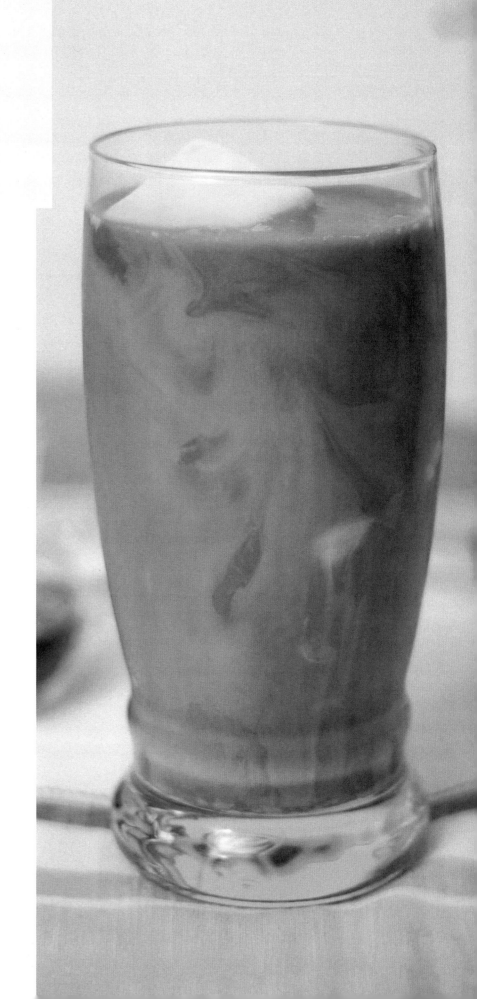

MATCHA LATTE

Servings: 1

Prep time: 5 minutes

Cook time: None

Wait time: None

What You'll Need:

- ½-1 teaspoon matcha powder
- 1 cup water
  + 2 tablespoons water
- ½ cup milk
- 2-3 teaspoons raw honey or maple syrup
- ⅛ teaspoon vanilla extract, optional

What To Do:

1. Add matcha powder and 2 tablespoons of water to a cup. Stir or whisk until thoroughly combined.
2. Add remaining cup of hot or cold water.
3. Add honey and stir until thoroughly combined.
4. Add ice if applicable.
5. Top with milk and serve immediately.

HONEY CINNAMON COFFEE

Servings: 1

Prep time: 4 minutes

Cook time: None

Wait time: None

What You'll Need:

- 1 cup freshly brewed organic coffee, any roast
- ½ cup milk
- 2-3 teaspoons raw honey
- ¼ teaspoon ground cinnamon
- ½ tablespoon butter, optional
- Ice cubes, optional

What To Do:

1. Add coffee to a 12-16 oz glass or mug. Add honey and cinnamon, and stir or whisk until completely combined.
2. Add butter if desired. Do not use butter if adding ice.
3. Add ice if applicable.
4. Froth milk in a separate glass using a frothing whisk or blend in a blender for 10-15 seconds.
5. Pour frothed milk over coffee and serve immediately.

MANGO DELIGHT SHAKE

Servings:
2-3

Prep time:
10 minutes

Cook time:
None

Wait time:
None

What You'll Need:

- 2 cups milk
- 2-4 tablespoons vanilla or unflavored protein powder
- 1 cup frozen mango chunks
- 1 ripe banana
- ½ cup frozen cauliflower
- ½ cup carrot
- 1 can (15 oz) pumpkin puree
- ½ cup unsweetened coconut cream
- 2 tablespoons hemp hearts
- ½ teaspoon ground cinnamon
- ½ teaspoon vanilla extract
- ½ teaspoon ground turmeric, optional

What To Do:

1. Add all ingredients to a high-powered blender and blend on high until mixture is smooth.

2. For a thinner shake, add an additional ¼-½ cup of milk and blend until desired consistency is achieved.

TIP: Riper bananas have a sweeter taste. If you have an under-ripened banana, preheat the oven to 350°F.

Place a banana (peel on) on a sheet pan, and bake for 7 minutes or until the peel is mostly brown.

Remove from the oven and allow to cool 2-3 minutes before peeling. The banana will be soft and perfectly sweet!

SOUPS

NOTES:

Any of our soups can be cooked on the stovetop in a dutch oven rather than a stock pot.

Soups are great slow cook dishes. If using this method, add all ingredients to a slow cooker, cover and cook for 6-8 hours on low or until any meat is cooked through and any veggies are fork tender.

WHITE CHICKEN CHILI

Servings:	Prep time:	Cook time:	Wait time:
6-8	30 minutes	40-45 minutes	10 minutes

What You'll Need:

- 1 pound chicken breasts
- 32 oz chicken broth
- 3 cans (15 oz) white beans, drained
- 1 small onion
- 2 Roma tomatoes
- 1 jalapeño or poblano pepper
- 3-4 cloves garlic
- 2 teaspoons ground cumin
- 2 teaspoons sea salt
- 1 teaspoon dried oregano
- ½ teaspoon cayenne powder
- ¼ cup fresh cilantro
- 2 tablespoons butter
- ¼ cup green onion, optional

What To Do:

1. Dice onion and tomatoes. Finely dice pepper. Mince garlic.
2. Heat a stock pot over medium heat. When the pot is hot, add butter.
3. Add diced veggies and garlic. Cook, stirring occasionally, for 10-12 minutes or until onion and pepper become soft.
4. Add chicken breasts, beans, broth, dried herbs, and spices. Stir to combine.
5. Bring to a rolling boil over medium-high heat. Continue to boil for 10-15 minutes or until chicken is cooked through.
6. Reduce heat to medium-low, remove chicken breasts and allow them to cool 1-2 minutes. Dice chicken into small pieces or pull apart into shreds using two forks.
7. Add 1 cup of the chili mixture (including beans and veggies) to a high powered blender and blend on high until mixture is smooth.
8. Add blended mixture and chicken back to the pot.
9. Finely dice cilantro and green onion. Add to the pot and stir to combine.
10. Cover and cook for 10-15 additional minutes.
11. Remove pot from the heat, and allow the soup to rest for 10 minutes before serving.

MEXICAN THREE BEAN SOUP

Servings:
6-8

Prep time:
12 minutes

Cook time:
1 hour 10 minutes

Wait time:
10 minutes

What You'll Need:

- 1 can (15 oz) black beans, drained
- 2 cans (15 oz) dark red kidney beans, drained
- 1 can (15 oz) chickpeas, drained
- 1 pound cooked ground beef, optional*
- 2 tablespoons butter
- 64 oz tomato juice
- 1 medium bell pepper
- 1 small red onion
- 1 large tomato
- 3-5 cloves garlic
- ⅓ cup fresh cilantro
- 1 teaspoon sea salt, or to taste
- 1 teaspoon black pepper, or to taste
- 1-2 tablespoons chili powder

What To Do:

1. Dice tomato and set aside. Dice red onion and bell pepper. Mince garlic.

2. In a stock pot, melt butter over medium heat. Add red onion, bell pepper, and garlic. Cook, stirring frequently, for 5 minutes or until veggies are mostly soft.

3. Add beans, chickpeas, diced tomato, tomato juice, and spices. Stir and bring to a rolling boil over medium-high heat. Continue to boil for 15 minutes, stirring frequently.

4. Reduce heat to medium-low, cover, and cook for 40-45 minutes, stirring occasionally.

5. Add ground beef and additional spices if applicable. Stir to combine.

6. Roughly chop cilantro, add it to the pot, and cook for 5 minutes uncovered, stirring frequently.

7. Remove pot from the heat, and allow the soup to rest for 10 minutes before serving.

*If ground beef is unseasoned, increase recipe seasonings by half of the listed measurement. Example: If the listed amount is 1 teaspoon, you would increase it to 1 ½ teaspoons.

CHICKEN COCONUT CURRY

Servings:	Prep time:	Cook time:	Wait time:
6-8	30 minutes	30 minutes	10 minutes

What You'll Need:

- 1 pound chicken breasts
- 32 oz chicken bone broth or chicken broth
- 1 can unsweetened coconut cream
- 2 cups kale
- 3 stalks celery
- 2 small onions
- 4 carrots
- 5 cloves garlic
- 2 cups mushrooms
- 2-4 tablespoons curry powder
- ½ teaspoon cayenne powder, optional
- 2 teaspoons sea salt, or to taste
- 2 tablespoons cooking oil

What To Do:

1. Cut chicken breasts in half, place into a medium saucepan, and cover with water. Bring to a rolling boil over high heat. Then, reduce heat to medium and simmer for 8 minutes.

2. While chicken is cooking, dice celery, onions, carrots, and mushrooms into ¼ inch pieces. Mince garlic. Finely chop kale.

3. Remove the saucepan from the heat and allow the chicken to rest. Chicken will continue to cook once added to soup.

4. Heat a stock pot over medium heat. When the pot is hot, add oil.

5. Add celery, onion, carrots, garlic, and mushrooms. Cook covered for 5 minutes, stirring occasionally.

6. Add seasonings and stir to combine. Cook uncovered for 5 minutes or until carrots are fork tender.

7. While veggies are cooking, dice chicken into small pieces or pull apart into shreds using two forks.

8. Add chicken, broth, kale and coconut cream to the pot and simmer for 5-8 minutes.

9. Add additional curry powder, salt, or broth to suit your taste preferences and allow to simmer for 3-5 minutes.

10. Remove pot from the heat, and allow the soup to rest for 10 minutes before serving.

Note: If using a slow cooker, chicken does not need to be cooked in advance. Add whole chicken breasts to the slow cooker. When breasts are fully cooked through, remove them from soup, chop or shred, and return to the soup.

LEMON WHITE BEAN SOUP

Servings:	Prep time:	Cook time:	Wait time:
4-6	20 minutes	35 minutes	10 minutes

What You'll Need:

- 3 cans (15 oz) cannellini beans, drained
- 2 cans (15 oz) chickpeas, drained
- 32 oz chicken bone broth
- 1 pound cooked, shredded chicken, optional*
- 2 large yellow carrots
- 1 medium yellow onion
- 2-3 cloves garlic
- 3 moderately packed cups green kale
- 2 tablespoons butter
- ½ tablespoon sea salt, or to taste
- 1 teaspoon black pepper
- 1 teaspoon dried rosemary
- 1 tablespoon dried parsley
- Zest and juice of half a lemon

What To Do:

1. Finely chop onion and carrots. Mince garlic. Roughly chop kale and set aside.
2. Blend 1 can of cannellini beans, 1 can of chickpeas, salt, pepper, and broth until smooth. Set aside for later.
3. In a stock pot, melt butter over medium-high heat.
4. Add carrots, onions, and garlic. Cook, stirring frequently, for 5-6 minutes or until onions become translucent and carrots begin to soften.
5. Reduce heat to medium-low, add kale, and stir. Cook for 2-3 additional minutes or until kale is fully wilted.
6. Add broth mixture, remaining cannellini beans, chickpeas, parsley and rosemary to the pot. Stir to combine and bring to a rolling boil over medium-high heat. Continue to boil for 10-12 minutes, stirring occasionally.
7. Remove the pot from the heat. If applicable, add chicken and additional spices.
8. Add lemon zest and lemon juice. Stir to combine.
9. Allow the soup to rest for 10 minutes before serving.

*If chicken is unseasoned, increase recipe seasonings by half of the listed measurement. Example: If the listed amount is 1 teaspoon, you would increase it to 1 ½ teaspoons.

Note: If using a slow cooker, make sure to complete steps 1 and 2 before adding ingredients to the slow cooker.

CHICKEN VEGGIE LENTIL SOUP

Servings:	Prep time:	Cook time:	Wait time:
6-8	15-20 minutes	35-40 minutes	10 minutes

What You'll Need:

- 1 pound chicken breasts
- 1 cup lentils
- 1 large onion
- 4 cloves garlic
- 2 medium carrots
- 4 stalks celery
- 1 can (15 oz) diced tomatoes, with liquid
- 2 moderately packed cups baby spinach
- 32 oz chicken broth
- ½ teaspoon ground cumin
- ½ teaspoon ground coriander
- ½ teaspoon ground turmeric
- ½ teaspoon smoked paprika
- ½ teaspoon black pepper
- 1 teaspoon sea salt, or to taste
- 1 tablespoon cooking oil

What To Do:

1. Dice onion, carrot, and celery. Mince garlic.
2. Heat a stock pot over medium heat. When the pot is hot, add oil. Add onion, garlic, carrots, celery, and all spices. Stir to combine. Cook for 8 minutes, stirring occasionally.
3. Add lentils, diced tomatoes, broth, and chicken breasts. Stir to combine.
4. Bring to a rolling boil over high heat. Then, reduce heat to medium and simmer for 15 minutes or until chicken is cooked through.
5. Remove chicken breasts and allow them to cool for 1-2 minutes. Dice chicken into small pieces or pull apart into shreds using two forks.
6. Continue to cook for 10 minutes or until lentils are soft.
7. Once lentils are cooked, add chicken back in.
8. Add spinach, stir to combine, and cook for 1-2 minutes.
9. Remove pot from the heat, and allow the soup to rest for 10 minutes before serving.

LEFTOVER POT ROAST SOUP

Servings:	Prep time:	Cook time:	Wait time:
4-6	10 minutes	20-25 minutes	10 minutes

What You'll Need:

- 2 cups cooked chuck roast
- 16 oz beef broth
- 1 medium onion
- 1-2 medium carrots
- 1-2 cloves garlic
- 1 can (15 oz) diced tomatoes, with liquid
- 10 oz bag frozen green peas
- 1 tablespoon Italian seasoning (pg 34)
- ½ teaspoon sea salt, or to taste
- ½-¾ teaspoon black pepper
- 1 tablespoon cooking oil

What To Do:

1. Dice onion, mince garlic, and slice carrots. Dice pot roast into small pieces or pull apart into shreds using two forks.

2. Heat a stock pot over medium-high heat. When the pot is hot, add oil.

3. Add onion, garlic, and carrots. Cook for 3-5 minutes, stirring occasionally.

4. Add all seasonings and cook for 5 minutes, stirring occasionally.

5. Add all remaining ingredients and stir to combine.

6. Reduce heat to medium-low, cover, and simmer for 10-15 minutes.

7. Remove pot from the heat, and allow the soup to rest for 10 minutes before serving.

Note: If using a slow cooker, cooked pot roast should be added 30 minutes before serving.

RED LENTIL SOUP

Servings:	Prep time:	Cook time:	Wait time:
3-4	10-12 minutes	40 minutes	10 minutes

What You'll Need:

- 1 cup red lentils
- 16 oz chicken broth
- ½-1 cup water
- 1 medium onion
- 1 large carrot
- 1 can (15 oz) diced tomatoes, drained
- 2 lightly packed cups baby spinach
- 2 cloves garlic
- 2 teaspoons ground cumin
- 2 teaspoons ground coriander
- 1 teaspoon ground turmeric
- ¾ teaspoon sea salt
- ½ teaspoon black pepper
- ⅛ teaspoon cayenne powder
- ⅛ teaspoon ground ginger
- 2 tablespoons butter
- 1 tablespoon cooking oil

What To Do:

1. Finely dice onion, carrot, and garlic. Roughly chop spinach.
2. Heat a stock pot over medium heat. When the pot is hot, add oil.
3. Add onion, carrot, and garlic. Cook for 2-3 minutes.
4. Add all spices to the pot and cook for 2 additional minutes.
5. Add lentils, broth, and tomatoes. Stir to combine.
6. Bring to a rolling boil over medium-high heat. Then, reduce heat to medium-low and cover. Simmer, stirring occasionally, for 30 minutes or until lentils are cooked through and creamy.
7. If the soup is getting too thick for your preference, add ¼ cup water at a time until desired consistency is achieved.
8. Add spinach, stir, and cook for 2 minutes.
9. Remove pot from the heat, and allow the soup to rest for 10 minutes before serving.
10. Spoon soup into bowls and top with butter.

EVERYTHING SOUP

Servings:	Prep time:	Cook time:	Wait time:
4-6	30 minutes	45 minutes	10 minutes

What You'll Need:

- 64 oz tomato juice
- 1 small eggplant
- 1 zucchini
- 3 stalks celery
- 3 small beets
- 1 tightly packed cup baby spinach
- 2 loosely packed cups kale
- 1 small yellow onion
- 4 tablespoons butter
- ½ tablespoon fresh cilantro (pg 7)
- 1 teaspoon garlic powder
- 1 teaspoon chili powder
- 1 teaspoon dried oregano
- 1 teaspoon sea salt, or to taste
- 1 teaspoon black pepper

What To Do:

1. Dice eggplant, zucchini, celery, and beets into bite-sized pieces. Finely dice onion, and cilantro. Roughly chop spinach and kale.

2. Melt butter in a stock pot over medium heat.

3. Add diced beets. Cover and cook for 2-3 minutes.

4. Add diced eggplant, zucchini, celery, and onion. Cover and cook for 3-4 minutes.

5. Add spinach and kale. Stir to combine. Re-cover and cook for 2-3 minutes.

6. Add dried herbs, spices, and tomato juice. Stir to combine.

7. Bring to a rolling boil over medium-high heat. Continue to boil for 15 minutes, stirring occasionally.

8. Reduce heat to medium-low and cover. Simmer, stirring occasionally, for 20 minutes or until veggies are fork tender.

9. Add cilantro and stir to combine.

10. Remove pot from the heat, and allow the soup to rest for 10 minutes before serving.

CREAMY PUMPKIN CHILI

Servings:	**Prep time:**	**Cook time:**	**Wait time:**
6-8	15 minutes	40 minutes	10 minutes

What You'll Need:

- 1 pound ground beef
- 1 medium butternut squash
- 1 can (15 oz) pumpkin puree
- 2 cans (15 oz) black beans, drained
- 1 can (15 oz) diced tomatoes, drained
- 16 oz chicken bone broth
- 16 oz tomato juice
- 2 teaspoons sea salt
- 1 ½ teaspoons black pepper
- 1 ½ teaspoons garlic powder
- 1 ½ teaspoons ground cumin
- 1 teaspoon curry powder
- 1 teaspoon chili powder
- 1 teaspoon smoked paprika
- 1 teaspoon onion powder
- 1 teaspoon ground turmeric
- 1 tablespoon cooking oil

What To Do:

1. Peel and dice butternut squash into bite-sized pieces.
2. Heat a stock pot over medium heat. When the pot is hot, add oil.
3. Add ground beef and cook, stirring frequently, for 5 minutes or until meat is broken up and mostly cooked.
4. Add black beans, butternut squash, and spices. Stir to combine.
5. Add remaining ingredients and stir to combine.
6. Bring to a rolling boil over medium-high heat. Continue to boil for 15 minutes, stirring occasionally.
7. Reduce heat to medium-low and simmer for 10 minutes or until butternut squash is fork tender.
8. Remove pot from the heat, and allow the soup to rest for 10 minutes before serving.

Note: If using a slow cooker, break apart uncooked ground beef into small pieces before adding.

SALADS

TOMATO BASIL CUCUMBER SALAD

Servings:	Prep time:	Cook time:	Wait time:
4-6	10 minutes	None	1 hour

What You'll Need:

- 3 medium tomatoes
- 2 cucumbers
- 1-2 tablespoons red onion, optional
- 3-4 tablespoons apple cider vinegar
- 2 tablespoons olive oil
- 3 tablespoons fresh basil
- 1-2 teaspoons sea salt
- 1-2 teaspoons black pepper

What To Do:

1. Dice tomatoes, cucumber, and onion into bite-sized pieces. Finely chop basil.

2. Add all ingredients to a bowl and toss to combine.

3. Refrigerate at least 1 hour or until ready to serve. Refrigerate overnight for maximum depth of flavor.

4. Leftovers can be stored in a sealed container in the refrigerator for up to 5 days.

ZESTY KALE SALAD

Servings:	**Prep time:**	**Cook time:**	**Wait time:**
2-4	15 minutes	None	5 minutes

What You'll Need:

- 5 moderately packed cups kale
- 1 medium carrot
- 1 medium apple
- 2 tablespoons cold oil
- 1 tablespoon red wine vinegar
- 2 teaspoons lemon juice*
- ⅛ teaspoon sea salt
- ⅛ cup pumpkin or sunflower seeds
- ¼ cup grated parmesan cheese
- ½-1 cup chicken, optional

What To Do:

1. Remove spines from kale and roughly chop or use pre-chopped kale. Grate carrot and finely dice apple.
2. Place chopped kale into a large bowl and add salt.
3. Grab a handful of kale, squeeze, and release. Repeat this until all of the kale is softened and dark green.
4. Add oil, vinegar, lemon juice, carrot, apple, and sunflower seeds to the bowl. Stir to combine.
5. Allow salad to rest for 5 minutes.
6. Add parmesan cheese and chicken. Stir to combine.

*If you are using a fresh lemon, you can also use zest of lemon as a garnish or combine with oil, vinegar, and lemon juice mixture.

FRESH VEGGIE QUINOA SALAD

Servings:	Prep time:	Cook time:	Wait time:
3-5	25 minutes	18 minutes	None

What You'll Need:

- 1 cup quinoa
- 2 cups water
- 1 bell pepper
- 3 mini cucumbers or 1 regular cucumber
- ½ loosely packed cup fresh cilantro
- 1-2 stalks celery
- 2 medium carrots
- 3 tablespoons cold oil
- 1 tablespoon lemon juice
- 2 tablespoons red wine vinegar
- ½ teaspoon sea salt
- ½ teaspoon black pepper
- ½ teaspoon garlic powder

Optional Additions:

- Diced red onion
- Diced tomatoes
- Chopped baby spinach

What To Do:

1. Thoroughly rinse quinoa under cool water and drain using a fine mesh strainer.
2. Add quinoa and water to a medium saucepan. Stir to combine.
3. Bring to a rolling boil over high heat. Then, reduce heat to low, cover, and simmer for 10 minutes.
4. Stir quinoa, re-cover, and continue to cook for 5 minutes.
5. Remove the saucepan from the heat and allow the quinoa to rest, covered, for 3 minutes.
6. Fluff quinoa with a fork and allow to fully cool.
7. While quinoa is cooling, finely dice veggies and cilantro.
   TIP: You can utilize a food processor to dice your veggies faster.
8. Add diced veggies, cilantro, oil and spices to a large bowl. Stir until veggies are thoroughly coated.
9. Add fully cooled quinoa and mix until thoroughly combined.
10. Serve immediately or refrigerate and serve cold.
11. Leftovers can be stored in a sealed container in the refrigerator for up to 4 days.

BAJA TACO SALAD

Servings:	Prep time:	Cook time:	Wait time:
4	30 minutes	20 minutes	None

What You'll Need:

Layer 1 - Base Salad Layer:

- 1-2 tightly packed cups shredded lettuce, cabbage, or baby spinach

Layer 2 - Taco Mixture:

- 1 pound ground beef
- ½ medium onion
- 1 medium bell pepper
- 1 cup black or pinto beans
- 4-5 cloves garlic
- 1 teaspoon chili powder
- ¾ teaspoon sea salt, or to taste
- ½ teaspoon black pepper, or to taste
- ½ teaspoon ground cumin
- 1 tablespoon cooking oil

Layer 3 - Cilantro Lime Cauliflower Rice:

- 10-12 oz bag cauliflower rice
- 1 lime
- 2 tablespoons fresh cilantro (pg 7)
- ¼ teaspoon sea salt
- 1-2 tablespoons cooking oil

Layer 4 - Optional Toppings:

- ¼ cup grated cheese
- 1 avocado
- 3-4 tablespoons fresh salsa (pg 90)

What To Do:

1. Dice onion and bell pepper. Mince garlic. Finely dice cilantro. Juice lime.

2. Heat a medium skillet over medium heat. When the skillet is hot, add 1 tablespoon of oil.

3. Add cauliflower rice and cook for 5 minutes or until tender. Add additional oil only if cauliflower rice begins to stick.

4. Add lime juice, cilantro, and salt. Stir, reduce heat to medium-low, and simmer for 2-3 minutes. Remove skillet from the heat and allow to cool.

5. Heat a large skillet over medium-high heat. When the skillet is hot, add 1 tablespoon of oil.

6. Add onions and peppers. Cook, stirring occasionally for 5-7 minutes or until veggies start to become translucent.

7. Add ground beef and garlic. Continue to cook, stirring frequently, for 5-7 minutes or until meat is broken up and thoroughly cooked.

8. Add beans and seasonings. Stir, reduce heat to medium-low, and simmer for 2-3 minutes.

9. Peel and pit avocado, and dice to desired size.

10. Layer serving dish as listed: base salad layer, taco mixture, cilantro lime cauliflower rice, and optional toppings.

SWEET POTATO, FETA, NUT SALAD

Servings:	Prep time:	Cook time:	Wait time:
2-4	15-20 minutes	20-25 minutes	None

What You'll Need:

- 1 large sweet potato
- ¼ teaspoon smoked paprika
- ¼ teaspoon garlic powder
- ¼ teaspoon sea salt, or to taste
- ⅛ teaspoon black pepper
- 1 tablespoon cooking oil
- 4 cups lettuce, baby spinach, or mixed greens
- ¼ cup feta cheese
- ¼ cup pecans or walnuts
- Balsamic vinaigrette, to taste (pg 93)

What To Do:

1. Preheat the oven to 400°F.
2. Peel and dice sweet potato into bite-sized pieces.
3. Add sweet potato, oil, and spices to a sheet pan. Stir until sweet potato pieces are thoroughly coated.
4. Bake for 20 minutes or until the sweet potato is cooked through and a little crispy.
5. Remove from the oven, transfer to a bowl or cold tray to cool completely.
6. While the sweet potato is cooling, roughly chop greens, crumble feta cheese, and crush or roughly chop nuts.
7. Add greens, cheese, and nuts to a large bowl.
8. Once sweet potato pieces are cool, add them to the bowl. Stir to combine.
9. Top with dressing and serve.

NUTTY APPLE CHICKEN SALAD

Servings:	Prep time:	Cook time:	Wait time:
4-6	15-20 minutes	15-20 minutes	10 minutes

What You'll Need:

- 1 pound chicken breasts
- ½ small onion
- 4 stalks celery
- 1 small apple
- 1 medium carrot
- ½-¾ cup raw unsalted cashews
- 1 cup avocado mayonnaise
- 1 teaspoon dried parsley
- ¾ teaspoon sea salt, or to taste
- ¼-½ teaspoon cayenne powder, optional

What To Do:

1. Add chicken breasts to a medium pot and cover with water. Bring water to a rolling boil over high heat.

2. Reduce heat to medium and simmer for 10 minutes or until chicken is cooked through.

3. While chicken is cooking, finely dice onion, celery, and apple. Grate or finely shred carrot. Crush or chop cashews.*

4. Remove pot from the heat. Remove chicken breasts from the water and allow them to cool for 10 minutes.

5. For a milder onion taste, cook onion over medium-high heat for 2-3 minutes before adding to mixture.

6. Dice chicken into small pieces or pull apart into shreds using two forks.*

7. Add all ingredients to a large bowl and mix until thoroughly combined.

8. Serve immediately or refrigerate and serve cold.

9. Leftovers can be stored in a sealed container in the refrigerator for up to 3 days.

*If you prefer a finer consistency, you can add all ingredients to a food processor and lightly pulse until desired texture is achieved.

SWEET HARVEST VEGGIE BAKE

Servings:	Prep time:	Cook time:	Wait time:
5-6	15-20 minutes	25-30 minutes	None

What You'll Need:

- 1 pound Brussels sprouts
- 2 large sweet potatoes
- 1 large onion
- ½-1 cup sunflower seeds
- 1 cup pitted Medjool dates
- 2 tablespoons cooking oil
- 2 tablespoons Mediterranean Spice Mix (pg 86) or seasoning blend of choice
- ½ teaspoon sea salt, or to taste

What To Do:

1. Preheat the oven to 350°F.

2. Peel and dice sweet potatoes and onions into bite-sized pieces. Remove the Brussels sprout stems and quarter them. Finely dice dates.

3. Add diced veggies, oil, and Mediterranean Spice Mix to a large sheet pan. Stir until veggies are thoroughly coated. Spread veggie mixture evenly across the pan.

4. Bake for 15 minutes.

5. Remove from the oven and sprinkle diced dates across the mixture.

6. Bake for 10-15 additional minutes or until veggies are fork tender.

7. Remove from the oven and sprinkle with sunflower seeds and salt to taste.

BUFFALO CAULIFLOWER

Servings:	Prep time:	Cook time:	Wait time:
4-6	10 minutes	25-30 minutes	None

What You'll Need:

- 1 head cauliflower
- 1 cup buffalo sauce*

What To Do:

1. Preheat the oven to 400°F.

2. Cut cauliflower into bite-sized pieces.

3. Add cauliflower and buffalo sauce to a large bowl. Stir until cauliflower is thoroughly coated. Spread cauliflower evenly across a walled sheet pan.

4. Bake for 25-30 minutes or until cauliflower is cooked and slightly browned on the edges.

*For a milder flavor, use ½ cup buffalo sauce combined with ½ cup ranch dressing or avocado mayonnaise.

CRISPY BAKED CABBAGE ROUNDS

Servings:	Prep time:	Cook time:	Wait time:
2-3	5-10 minutes	30-35 minutes	None

What You'll Need:

- 1 head cabbage*
- ½ teaspoon garlic powder
- ½ teaspoon smoked paprika
- ½ teaspoon sea salt, or to taste
- ¼ teaspoon black pepper, or to taste
- 2 tablespoons butter, sliced
- 1-2 tablespoons cooking oil

What To Do:

1. Preheat the oven to 350°F.

2. Slice cabbage into ¼-½ inch thick rounds, starting furthest from the stem. Slice enough to fill an oiled sheet pan in a single layer (typically about 6 slices).

3. Coat the top of each cabbage round with oil and spices.

4. Bake for 30 minutes or until cabbage is soft and beginning to crisp at the edges.

5. Remove from the oven and top with thin slices of butter.

6. *Depending on size, you may not use the entire cabbage.

BUTTERY SWEET POTATO MASH

Servings:	Prep time:	Cook time:	Wait time:
4-6	20 minutes	20-25 minutes	None

What You'll Need:

- 3 medium sweet potatoes
- 6 tablespoons butter
- ¼ cup milk, optional
- 1-2 tablespoons lemon juice, optional
- 1 teaspoon garlic powder
- ½ teaspoon sea salt, or to taste

What To Do:

1. Peel and chop sweet potatoes into 2-inch cubes. Place the cubes into a stock pot and cover with water.

2. Bring to a rolling boil over high heat. Then, reduce heat to medium-low and simmer for 20-25 minutes or until cubes are fork tender.

3. Drain water and add all remaining ingredients. Stir and mash with a fork or potato masher until potatoes reach your desired consistency.

TIP: For an extra creamy mash, pour mixture into a high-powered blender or food processor and add ¼ cup of milk.

CAJUN SWEET POTATO FRIES

Servings:	Prep time:	Cook time:	Wait time:
3-4	15 minutes	20-30 minutes	None

What You'll Need:

- 2 medium-large sweet potatoes
- 1 teaspoon smoked paprika
- 1 teaspoon garlic powder
- 1 teaspoon dried oregano
- ½ teaspoon onion powder
- ½ teaspoon sea salt, or to taste
- ¼ teaspoon black pepper
- ¼-½ teaspoon cayenne powder
- 2 tablespoons cooking oil

What To Do:

1. Preheat the oven to 450°F or air fryer to 400°F.

2. Peel and cut sweet potatoes into ¼-½ inch thick sticks.

3. Add sweet potato sticks, oil, herbs, and spices to a large sheet pan. Stir until sticks are thoroughly coated. Spread sweet potato sticks evenly across the pan.

4. Bake for 15-20 minutes or until fries reach your desired crispiness.

SPINACH ARTICHOKE DIP

Servings:
6-8

Prep time:
10-15 minutes

Cook time:
25-30 minutes

Wait time:
None

What You'll Need:

- 32-36 oz artichoke hearts*
- 4 loosely packed cups baby spinach
- 2 cups avocado mayonnaise
- 1 cup grated parmesan cheese
- 1 teaspoon garlic powder
- 1 teaspoon onion powder
- 1 teaspoon smoked paprika
- ½ teaspoon chili powder
- ½ teaspoon sea salt, or to taste
- 4 tablespoons butter

What To Do:

1. Preheat the oven to 350°F.

2. Drain and dice artichoke hearts. Roughly chop spinach. Thinly slice butter.

3. Add all ingredients except butter to a medium-large baking dish and mix until thoroughly combined. Spread mixture evenly across the baking dish, and top with slices of butter.

4. Bake for 15 minutes.

5. Remove from the oven, stir, and spread mixture evenly.

6. Bake for 10 additional minutes or until artichoke hearts have fully softened and spinach is wilted.

7. Serve warm with celery, other dipping veggies, or grain-free chips.

*Look for artichoke hearts that are not in unhealthy oils or marinated with spices.

I CAN'T BELIEVE IT'S NUT CORNBREAD

Servings:	Prep time:	Cook time:	Wait time:
6-8	10-15 minutes	25 minutes	10 minutes

What You'll Need:

- 1 ½ cups almond flour
- ¼ cup cassava flour
- 5 eggs
- 2 teaspoons aluminum free baking powder
- 4 tablespoons melted butter
- ¼ cup milk (raw or almond)
- 1 teaspoon smoked paprika
- 1 teaspoon onion powder
- 1 teaspoon garlic powder
- 1 tablespoon dried parsley
- 1 teaspoon sea salt
- ½ teaspoon black pepper

What To Do:

1. Preheat the oven to 375°F.
2. Melt butter in a small saucepan over medium heat. Remove the saucepan from the heat and allow to cool for 5 minutes.
3. In a large bowl, beat eggs, milk, and butter together until thoroughly combined.
4. In a separate bowl, mix both flours, baking powder, herbs, and spices together.
5. Slowly mix dry and wet ingredients until thoroughly combined.
6. Pour mixture into an oiled 7x11 baking dish or small cast iron skillet and use a spatula to spread evenly.
7. Bake for 25 minutes or until mixture is cooked through and edges begin to crisp.
8. Remove from the oven and allow to rest 10 minutes prior to cutting.
9. Serve topped with sliced butter.

GARLIC LEMON GREEN BEANS

Servings:	Prep time:	Cook time:	Wait time:
3-4	5 minutes	15-20 minutes	None

What You'll Need:

· 1 pound green beans

· ⅓ lemon

· 3 cloves garlic

· ½ teaspoon sea salt, or to taste

· ½ teaspoon black pepper

· 1 tablespoon cooking oil

What To Do:

1. Thoroughly rinse green beans. Remove stems and strings if necessary. Mince garlic.

2. Heat a large skillet over medium heat. When the skillet is hot, add oil.

3. Add green beans and cook for 5 minutes.

4. Add garlic, salt, and pepper. Stir to combine. Cover and continue to cook, stirring frequently, for 15 minutes or until green beans are tender.

5. Zest lemon over the beans and top with a squeeze of fresh lemon juice.

TIP: Rolling a lemon a few times across the counter while pressing down with the palm of your hand makes juicing easier!

GARLIC PARMESAN BROCCOLI

Servings:
2-4

Prep time:
8 minutes

Cook time:
20 minutes

Wait time:
None

What You'll Need:

- 1 head broccoli
- ½ cup grated parmesan cheese
- 3 cloves garlic
- ½ teaspoon sea salt, or to taste
- 1 tablespoon cooking oil
- 1 small lemon, optional

What To Do:

1. Preheat the oven to 400°F.
2. Cut broccoli into bite-sized pieces. Mince garlic.
3. Add broccoli, garlic, oil, and salt to a medium-large glass or cast iron baking dish. Stir until broccoli is thoroughly coated, then spread evenly.
4. Bake for 20 minutes or until broccoli is fork tender and/or slightly browned.
5. Remove from the oven and immediately top with parmesan. Stir gently to combine.
6. For added flavor, top with a squeeze of fresh lemon juice.

HONEY BALSAMIC BRUSSELS SPROUTS

Servings:	Prep time:	Cook time:	Wait time:
4-5	10 minutes	20-25 minutes	None

What You'll Need:

- 1 pound Brussels sprouts
- ¼ cup raw honey
- ¼ cup balsamic vinegar
- 1 tablespoon dijon mustard
- 2 cloves garlic
- ¼ teaspoon sea salt, or to taste
- 3 tablespoon butter
- 1 tablespoon cooking oil

What To Do:

1. Preheat the oven to 425°F.

2. Remove the Brussels sprout stems and quarter or half them. Place onto a sheet pan and coat with oil and salt.

3. Bake for 20-25 minutes or until Brussels are fork tender and slightly crispy.

4. While Brussels are cooking, finely mince garlic.

5. Heat honey in a small saucepan over medium heat. Simmer for 1-2 minutes

6. Add balsamic vinegar, Dijon mustard, and garlic. Stir until thoroughly combined.

7. Add butter, reduce heat to medium-low and simmer for 4-5 minutes, stirring frequently to prevent burning.

8. Once Brussels sprouts are cooked through, remove from the oven.

9. Drizzle the Brussels sprouts with honey glaze and stir until thoroughly coated.

SWEET POTATO CASSEROLE

Servings:	Prep time:	Cook time:	Wait time:
8-10	20-25 minutes	50-55 minutes	5 minutes

What You'll Need:

Sweet Potato Mixture:

- 5-6 medium sweet potatoes
- 1 egg
- ⅓ cup unsweetened coconut cream (solid portion only)
- 2 tablespoons maple syrup
- 2 tablespoons butter
- 1 teaspoon vanilla extract
- ¼ teaspoon sea salt

Topping:

- ¾ cup unsweetened coconut shreds
- 1 cup pecan pieces
- 3 tablespoons maple syrup
- 4 tablespoons butter

What To Do:

1. Sweet Potato Mixture: Peel and chop sweet potatoes into large pieces. Place into a stock pot and cover with water.

2. Bring water to a rolling boil over high heat. Stir, reduce heat to medium, and simmer for 20-25 minutes or until potatoes are fork tender.

3. Drain water and add remaining sweet potato mixture ingredients. Stir and mash together with a fork or potato masher until potatoes reach desired consistency. **TIP:** You can also use a mixer if you have one available.

4. Preheat the oven to 350°F.

5. Transfer sweet potato mixture to a 8x8 baking dish and spread evenly.

6. Topping: Use a food processor or high-powered blender to pulse coconut shreds until fine. Combine coconut with pecan pieces and sprinkle mixture evenly across the sweet potato mixture.

7. Melt butter and mix together with maple syrup. Using a spoon, drizzle butter mixture evenly across the casserole.

8. Bake for 30 minutes.

9. Remove from the oven and allow to rest at least 5 minutes before serving.

DESSERTS & SNACKS

FRUITY CHIA PUDDING

Servings:	Prep time:	Cook time:	Wait time:
2	5-12 minutes	None	3+ hours

What You'll Need:

- 1 ½ cups milk
- 1 cup fresh fruit (berries, mango, or peaches are best)
- ½ cup chia seeds
- 1-2 tablespoons maple syrup
- ⅛-¼ teaspoon vanilla extract
- ⅛ teaspoon ground cinnamon

What To Do:

1. Add milk, maple syrup, vanilla, and ½ cup of fruit to a blender. Blend on high until mixture is smooth.

2. Pour mixture into a container with a lid. (Quart jars work great!) Add chia seeds and mix thoroughly until there are no clumps. (Chia seeds love to stick together.)

3. Cover container and refrigerate for 5 minutes. Stir or shake to redistribute liquid. Re-cover the container and refrigerate overnight or for at least 3 hours.

4. Dice or prepare remaining fruit. Transfer prepared fruit to a separate container, cover, and refrigerate until pudding is ready.

5. When you are ready to serve, top with remaining fruit and cinnamon.

6. Leftovers can be stored in a sealed container in the refrigerator for up to 4 days.

59

CHOCOLATE SOFT SERVE NICE CREAM

Servings:	Prep time:	Cook time:	Wait time:
3-4	10 minutes	None	20 minutes

What You'll Need:

- 2 ½ cups frozen avocado chunks
- 1 large ripe banana
- ¾ cup milk
- 4 tablespoons unsweetened cocoa powder
- 5-6 tablespoons maple syrup
- 1 teaspoon vanilla extract

Optional Toppings:

- Nuts*
- Cacao nibs*
- Shredded Coconut
- Banana slices

What To Do:

1. Add all ingredients to a high-powered blender or food processor and blend until smooth. If needed, use your blender's tamper accessory to keep the mixture from sticking to the sides during the blending process. If you don't have a tamper, periodically stop the blender and use a spatula to scrape sides.

2. If necessary, add additional milk 1 tablespoon at a time to achieve a smooth texture.

3. Transfer to a container and freeze for 20 minutes before serving.

4. Leftovers can be stored in a sealed container in the freezer. Contents will become completely hardened when frozen. Allow the mixture to thaw for 10-15 minutes before eating.

*Nuts and cacao nibs can be mixed into the nice cream prior to freezing or added with other toppings just prior to serving.

CHOCOLATE NUT BUTTER BANANA BITES

Servings:	Prep time:	Cook time:	Wait time:
8	20 minutes	10-15 minutes	2-3 hours

What You'll Need:

- 4 ripe bananas
- ⅓ cup nut butter, any variety*
- ¼ cup unsweetened cocoa powder
- ½ cup coconut oil
- ¼-⅓ cup maple syrup
- 1 teaspoon vanilla extract

What To Do:

1. Peel bananas and slice into ¼ inch thick rounds.**

2. Create mini sandwiches using 2 slices of banana with nut butter in the center and place onto a small, lightly oiled sheet pan. Stick a toothpick down through the center of each sandwich to prevent sliding.

3. Freeze 2 hours or until bananas are completely frozen.

4. When the sandwiches are almost frozen, prepare the chocolate sauce. In a small saucepan, heat coconut oil on medium-low heat until melted.

5. Add cocoa powder, maple syrup, and vanilla. Stir until mixture reaches a smooth consistency.

6. Remove the saucepan from the heat and allow to cool for 15-20 minutes or until mixture begins to thicken.

7. **TIP:** For more effective dipping, transfer chocolate mixture to a container with a small diameter such as a shot glass or 3-4 oz jar. This allows for better coverage and less waste.

8. Dip each banana sandwich into melted chocolate using the toothpick. Allow any excess chocolate to drip off, then transfer back to the sheet pan.

9. Freeze for 5-10 minutes to allow chocolate to harden.

10. If you have chocolate remaining, you can repeat the dip and freeze process.

11. Consume within 5 minutes of removing from the freezer.

12. Extra bites can be stored in a sealed container in the freezer for up to 1 month.

*We recommend using thicker, less oily nut butters. Our Mixed Nut Butter (pg 87) works great! If your nut butter is particularly oily or runny, you can add 1-2 tablespoons of flaxseed meal to create a thicker consistency that is easier to work with.

**IMPORTANT: Do not pre-freeze banana slices before adding nut butter. If you do, bananas will fall apart during the assembly process.

BAKED CINNAMON PEACHES
WITH COCONUT WHIPPED CREAM

Servings:	Prep time:	Cook time:	Wait time:
6-10	20 minutes	30 minutes	8 hours

What You'll Need:

Peaches:

- 3 large or 5 medium peaches*

- ¼ tablespoon ground cinnamon

- 2 tablespoons maple syrup

- 3 tablespoons butter

Coconut Cream:

- 1 can unsweetened coconut cream, chilled

- 2 tablespoons maple syrup

- 1 teaspoon vanilla extract

What To Do:

1. Refrigerate coconut cream for at least 8 hours.

2. Preheat the oven to 375°F.

3. Cut peaches in half and remove pits. Place peach halves cut side up on a sheet pan.

4. Drizzle each half with maple syrup, sprinkle with cinnamon, and top with a small slice of butter.

5. Bake for 30 minutes.

6. Remove peaches from the oven and allow to cool 3-4 minutes before plating.

7. While peaches are cooling, prepare the coconut whipped cream. A stand mixer or hand mixer is preferred for this process.

8. Remove coconut cream from the refrigerator - DO NOT SHAKE. Open the can, and carefully scoop only the solid portion into a mixing bowl. The liquid portion can be discarded or saved for other recipes.

9. Add maple syrup and vanilla to the mixing bowl.

10. Stand or Hand Mixer Method: Whip on medium-high for 3-4 minutes or until medium peaks form.

11. Hand Mixing Method: Thoroughly whisk mixture until smooth and slightly thickened. This method will not achieve a traditional whipped cream texture.

12. Spoon whipped cream onto the peach halves and serve immediately.

*Ripe but still slightly firm peaches work best for this recipe.

STRAWBERRY CASHEW CREAM PIE

Servings:	Prep time:	Cook time:	Wait time:
4-6	25 minutes	12-15 minutes	15-20 minutes

What You'll Need:

Crust:

- ½ cup almond flour
- ½ cup coconut flour
- ⅓ cup melted butter
- 2 teaspoons vanilla extract
- 1 egg
- 1 ½ teaspoon unsweetened cocoa powder
- 2-4 teaspoons raw honey or maple syrup

Filling:

- 2 ½ cups water
- 2 ½ cups raw unsalted cashews
- 10 pitted Medjool dates
- 1 teaspoon ground cinnamon
- ½ cup milk

Topping:

- ¾-1 cup strawberry jam (pg 88) or preserves
- 1-2 tablespoons raw unsalted cashews, optional

What To Do:

1. Preheat the oven to 375ºF.
2. In a medium bowl, use a fork to thoroughly combine crust ingredients.
3. Transfer mixture to a standard pie dish using your hands, and press to evenly distribute mixture across the bottom and sides.
4. Bake for 12-15 minutes or until crust edges begin to brown.
5. While the crust is baking, remove stems and pits from dates if necessary.
6. In a small pot, bring water to a rolling boil over high heat.
7. Add cashews and dates to a medium-large bowl. Add enough boiled water to just cover cashews and dates. Allow to soak for 10 minutes.
8. Drain water from bowl, and transfer softened cashews and dates to a high-powered blender or food processor.
9. Add milk and cinnamon and blend until smooth. The mixture should be thick so it will stay together when pie is cut. **Note:** This may take a few extra minutes depending on the quality of your blender. If the mixture begins to cling to the sides, use your blender's tamper accessory or pause the blender periodically and use a spatula to scrape the mixture back down into the blades. Only add additional milk, 1 tablespoon at a time, if it is absolutely necessary for blending.
10. Remove crust from the oven and allow to cool 5-10 minutes before filling.
11. Pour cashew filling into the crust and use a spatula to spread evenly. Freeze for 5 minutes to rapidly cool.
12. Remove from the freezer and use a spatula to spread strawberry preserves evenly on top of cashew filling.
13. Optional: Place the cashews for topping into a reusable snack bag or kitchen towel. Use a rolling pin or heavy object to crush cashews to your desired consistency. Sprinkle crushed cashews onto the pie.
14. Refrigerate until ready to eat.

PUMPKIN PECAN SHORTBREAD BARS

Servings:	Prep time:	Cook time:	Wait time:
8-10	25 minutes	1 hour 10 minutes	20 minutes

What You'll Need:

Shortbread:

- ½ cup almond flour
- ¾ cup cassava flour
- 1 egg
- ¼ cup milk
- 3 tablespoons melted butter
- 2 teaspoons vanilla extract
- 1 teaspoon aluminum free baking powder
- 2 teaspoons ground cinnamon
- ¼ teaspoon sea salt
- 3 teaspoons maple syrup

Pumpkin Mixture:

- 2 cans (15 oz) pumpkin puree
- 4 eggs
- 6 tablespoons maple syrup
- 4 teaspoons vanilla extract
- 1-2 tablespoons ground cinnamon
- ¾ teaspoon ground ginger
- ¾ teaspoon ground nutmeg
- ½ teaspoon sea salt

Topping:

- ¼-½ cup pecan pieces

What To Do:

1. Preheat the oven to 375°F.
2. Thoroughly combine shortbread ingredients in a large mixing bowl.
3. Press mixture evenly into a lightly oiled 9x13 baking dish. **Note:** Mixture will be very thin across the bottom.
4. Bake for 10 minutes.
5. In the mixing bowl, combine pumpkin mixture ingredients.
6. Remove the baking dish from the oven, pour pumpkin mixture over the crust, and gently shake the dish side to side to level the mixture.
7. Bake for 10 minutes.
8. Remove from the oven and sprinkle pecan pieces evenly across the top.
9. Bake for 50 minutes.
10. Remove from the oven and allow to rest at least 15 minutes before slicing.

COCO-NUT BUTTER ENERGY BALLS

Servings:	Prep time:	Cook time:	Wait time:
65 balls	10-20 minutes	None	45-50 minutes

What You'll Need:

- 4 ¾ cups unsweetened coconut shreds
- ½ cup hemp hearts
- ¼ cup flaxseed meal
- 26 oz nut butter (pg 87), any variety
- 1 cup raw honey
- ½ teaspoon vanilla extract
- ¼ teaspoon ground cinnamon

What To Do:

1. Set aside ¼ cup of coconut shreds to be used for topping.
2. Add all remaining ingredients to a stand mixer and mix until thoroughly combined.
3. If you don't have a mixer, use your hands to combine ingredients in a large mixing bowl. We recommend wearing disposable gloves to make mixing less messy.
4. Cover the mixing bowl and refrigerate for 15-20 minutes or until mixture is chilled.
5. Form dough into 1" balls and place on a small, lightly oiled sheet pan.
6. Top with a sprinkle of coconut shreds.
7. Refrigerate uncovered at least 30 minutes to allow dough to firm.
8. Energy balls can be enjoyed immediately or frozen to make them more firm.
9. Extra bites can be stored in a sealed container in the freezer for up to 2 weeks.

PEPPERMINT PATTY BITES

Servings:
9 bites

Prep time:
15-20 minutes

Cook time:
None

Wait time:
30 minutes

What You'll Need:

- 8-10 pitted Medjool dates
- 1 cup raw unsalted cashews
- 2 tablespoons cacao nibs
- 2 tablespoons unsweetened cocoa powder
- 1 tablespoon nut butter
- 1 tablespoon maple syrup
- ¼ teaspoon peppermint extract
- 2 tablespoons hot water

What To Do:

1. Add dates, cashews, and cacao nibs to a high-powered blender or food processor. Blend on high until mixture becomes a coarse powder.

2. If the mixture begins to cling to the sides, use your blender's tamper accessory or pause the blender periodically and use a spatula to scrape the mixture back down into the blades.

3. Add all ingredients to a stand mixer and mix until thoroughly combined.

4. If you don't have a mixer, use your hands to combine ingredients in a large mixing bowl. We recommend wearing disposable gloves to make mixing less messy.

5. If dough doesn't stick together, add additional water 1 tablespoon at a time until the dough properly combines.

6. Form dough into 1" balls and place on a plate or small sheet pan. Refrigerate at least 30 minutes to allow dough to firm.

7. Extra bites can be stored in a sealed container in the freezer for up to 2 weeks.

MISCELLANEOUS

PERFECTLY COOKED QUINOA

Servings:	Prep time:	Cook time:	Wait time:
3-4	2 minutes	15 minutes	3 minutes

What You'll Need:

- 1 cup quinoa
- 16 oz broth (pg 18) or water
- 1 tablespoon seasoning blend of choice*
- 1 tablespoon butter

What To Do:

1. Thoroughly rinse quinoa under cool water and drain using a fine mesh strainer.
2. Add quinoa and broth to a medium saucepan. Stir to combine.
3. Bring to a rolling boil over high heat. Then, reduce heat to low, cover, and simmer for 10 minutes.
4. Stir quinoa, re-cover, and continue to cook for 5 minutes.
5. Remove the saucepan from the heat and allow the quinoa to rest, covered, for 3 minutes.
6. Add seasonings and butter, and fluff quinoa with a fork to combine.

*We recommend using a seasoning blend such as Italian Seasoning (pg 34), Taco Seasoning (pg 33), or Mediterranean Spice Mix (pg 86). If you don't have a preferred seasoning blend, you can go with the classic trio: 1 teaspoon each of sea salt, black pepper, and garlic powder.

MEDITERRANEAN SPICE MIX

Servings:	Prep time:	Cook time:	Wait time:
1/4 cup	5-10 minutes	None	None

What You'll Need:

- 1 tablespoon garlic powder
- 1 tablespoon smoked paprika
- 2 teaspoons sea salt
- 1 teaspoon onion powder
- 1 teaspoon black pepper
- 1 teaspoon dried oregano
- 1 teaspoon ground cumin
- ½ teaspoon dried thyme
- ½ teaspoon ground turmeric
- ¼ teaspoon dried basil
- ¼ teaspoon dried cilantro
- ¼ teaspoon dried parsley
- ¼ teaspoon ground coriander

What To Do:

1. Combine and store in a sealed container.

MIXED NUT BUTTER

Servings:	Prep time:	Cook time:	Wait time:
3-4 cups	10-15 minutes	None	None

What You'll Need:

- 4 cups nuts (cashews, almonds, pecans, walnuts, hazelnut)
- 1 cup unsweetened coconut shreds
- ⅔ cup avocado oil
- ¼ teaspoon sea salt, or to taste
- 1 teaspoon vanilla extract, optional
- 1-2 teaspoons raw honey, optional

What To Do:

1. Add nuts and coconut shreds to a high-powered blender or food processor. Blend until nuts are finely chopped and well mixed.

2. Add avocado oil and optional ingredients.

3. Continue blending until the mixture is a smooth consistency. If the mixture begins to cling to the sides, use your blender's tamper accessory or pause the blender periodically and use a spatula to scrape the mixture back down into the blades.

4. Note: Depending on the strength and speed of your blender or processor, it may take longer to achieve desired texture. Stick with the process at least 10 minutes before adding extra oil. The more the nuts are processed, the more natural oil they will release.

5. Nut butter can be stored in a sealed container in the refrigerator for up to 2 months or in the freezer for up to 6 months.

STRAWBERRY CHIA JAM

Servings:
1 pint

Prep time:
5 minutes

Cook time:
20 minutes

Wait time:
10 minutes

What You'll Need:

- 1 pound fresh strawberries
- 2 tablespoons maple syrup
- 3 tablespoons chia seeds

What To Do:

1. Remove leaves and stems from the strawberries.

2. Add strawberries to a high-powered blender or food processor. Blend on high until they reach a smooth, liquid consistency.

3. Add puréed strawberries and maple syrup to a medium saucepan. Stir to combine.

4. Bring to a low boil over medium heat. Then, reduce heat to medium-low and simmer for 5 minutes, stirring frequently.

5. Remove the saucepan from the heat and stir in chia seeds until thoroughly combined.

6. Return saucepan to the heat, reduce heat to low, and simmer for 15 minutes, stirring occasionally.

7. Serve warm or transfer mixture to a jar and refrigerate for 10 minutes to achieve ideal consistency.

8. Chia jam can be stored in a sealed container in the refrigerator for up to 2 weeks.

SMOKED SALMON HUMMUS

Servings:	**Prep time:**	**Cook time:**	**Wait time:**
6-8	10-15 minutes	None	None

What You'll Need:

- 4 oz smoked salmon*
- 2 cans (15 oz) chickpeas, drained
- 1 tablespoon sesame seeds
- 1 teaspoon garlic powder
- 1 teaspoon black pepper
- 1 teaspoon onion powder
- 1 teaspoon smoked paprika
- 1 teaspoon sea salt, or to taste
- 1 teaspoon dried parsley
- 2-3 tablespoons lemon juice
- ½ cup cold oil

What To Do:

1. Add all ingredients except salmon to a high-powered blender or food processor.

2. Start the blender on low and slowly increase speed until mixture is a smooth consistency.

3. If the mixture begins to cling to the sides, use your blender's tamper accessory or pause the blender periodically and use a spatula to scrape the mixture back down into the blades.

4. Add smoked salmon to the mixture. Pulse in short bursts until salmon is broken into small pieces.

5. Transfer to a large bowl and refrigerate until ready to serve.

6. Leftover hummus can be stored in a sealed container in the refrigerator for up to 3 days.

*Smoked salmon often has added flavors, colors, and sugars. Check ingredients and make sure it only contains wild-caught salmon and salt.

FRESH HOMEMADE SALSA

Servings:	**Prep time:**	**Cook time:**	**Wait time:**
1.5 quarts	20-25 minutes	20 minutes	None

What You'll Need:

- 5 Roma tomatoes
- 1 can (15 oz) diced tomatoes, drained
- 1 large poblano pepper*
- 1 medium-large bell pepper
- 1 small red onion
- 3-4 cloves garlic
- 2 tablespoons green onion
- ⅓ cup fresh cilantro
- 1 tablespoon lime juice
- 1 ½ teaspoons sea salt, or to taste
- ½ teaspoon chili powder
- ½ teaspoon ground cumin
- ½ teaspoon black pepper
- ½ teaspoon cayenne powder, optional
- 1 tablespoon cooking oil

What To Do:

1. Remove stems and seeds from poblano and bell peppers. Roughly chop both peppers, garlic, and red onion. Cut green onion into large pieces. Core and quarter Roma tomatoes and discard the more juicy parts.

2. Heat a large skillet over medium heat. When the skillet is hot, add oil.

3. Add peppers and red onion. Cook, occasionally stirring, for 10 minutes or until translucent.

4. Increase heat to medium-high and continue to cook 2-3 minutes without stirring or until a char begins to form.

5. Add Roma tomatoes, green onion and garlic. Stir to combine.

6. Reduce heat to medium-low and continue to cook for 4-5 minutes, stirring frequently.

7. Remove the skillet from the heat. Pour cooked veggies, diced tomatoes, cilantro, lime juice, herbs, and spices into a high-powered blender or food processor. Pulse in quick bursts until salsa is your desired texture.

8. **TIP:** If you have an immersion blender, you can remove the skillet from the heat, add remaining ingredients and blend directly in the skillet.

9. Transfer salsa to a large bowl or jar and serve warm or refrigerate and serve cold.

10. Leftover salsa can be stored in a sealed container in the refrigerator for up to 3 days.

*For hotter salsa, use 2-3 jalapeños (with seeds for maximum spice) instead of poblano.

DRESSINGS & SAUCES

BUFFALO SAUCE

Servings:	Prep time:	Cook time:	Wait time:
2 cups	10 minutes	None	None

What You'll Need:

- 1 cup red hot sauce*

- ½ cup oil

- 2 tablespoons white wine vinegar

- ½ teaspoon garlic powder

- 4-5 tablespoons cashew butter

- ½ teaspoon cayenne powder, optional for extra spice

What To Do:

1. Add all ingredients to a blender. Blend on high until ingredients are thoroughly combined.

2. Store in a sealed container in the refrigerator for up to 3 months.

*Use your preferred hot sauce that contains the following type of ingredients: cayenne or other hot red peppers, vinegar, salt, garlic. Green sauces do not work for this recipe. Do not use sauces that contain sugar or preservatives.

RANCH DRESSING

Servings:	Prep time:	Wait time:
2.5 cups	10 minutes	30 minutes

What You'll Need:

- 1 ½ cup avocado mayonnaise
- ¼ cup lemon juice
- ½ cup fresh parsley
- 2 tablespoons fresh dill (pg 7)
- 4-5 cloves garlic
- ½ teaspoon sea salt, or to taste
- ½ teaspoon black pepper, or to taste

What To Do:

1. Finely dice parsley and dill before measuring.
2. Add all ingredients to a blender. Blend on high until mixture is smooth.
3. Refrigerate 30 minutes before first use.
4. Store in a sealed container in the refrigerator for up to 1 month.

HONEY MUSTARD

Servings:	Prep time:	Wait time:
1.5 cups	5-10 minutes	None

What You'll Need:

- ½ cup oil
- ½ cup Dijon mustard
- 2-4 tablespoons raw honey
- 3 tablespoons apple cider vinegar
- 2 teaspoons lemon juice
- ¼ teaspoon sea salt
- ¼ teaspoon black pepper

What To Do:

1. Combine ingredients in a jar or bottle and shake until combined.
2. Store in a sealed container in the refrigerator for up to 3 months.

ITALIAN DRESSING

Servings:	Prep time:	Wait time:
1.5 cups	10 minutes	None

What You'll Need:

- 1 cup oil*
- ¼ cup lemon juice
- ¼ cup red wine vinegar
- 1 clove garlic
- ¾ teaspoon dried oregano
- ¾ teaspoon sea salt
- ½ teaspoon dried basil
- ½ teaspoon Italian seasoning (pg 34)
- ½ teaspoon mustard powder, optional
- ¼ teaspoon onion powder

What To Do:

1. Add all ingredients to a blender. Lightly blend until herbs are your desired size.
2. Store in a sealed container for up to 1 month.

*If you plan to use this as a marinade for meat or veggies, make sure to use an oil that is safe for cooking (pg 12).

BALSAMIC VINAIGRETTE

Servings:	Prep time:	Wait time:
1 cup	10 minutes	None

What You'll Need:

- ¾ cup oil
- ¼ cup balsamic vinegar
- ½ teaspoon sea salt, or to taste
- ½ teaspoon black pepper
- 1 teaspoon garlic powder
- 1 tablespoon dijon mustard
- ½-1 tablespoon raw honey, optional

What To Do:

1. Combine ingredients in a jar or bottle and shake until combined.
2. Store in a sealed container for up to 3 months.

CLASSIC KETCHUP

Servings:	Prep time:	Cook time:	Wait time:
1.5 cups	10 minutes	5 minutes	2 minutes

What You'll Need:

- 6 oz tomato paste
- ¾-1 cup water
- 1 tablespoon distilled white vinegar
- ½ teaspoon onion powder
- ¼ teaspoon garlic powder
- ½ teaspoon sea salt, or to taste
- 1 tablespoon maple syrup, optional

What To Do:

1. In a small saucepan, bring water to a rolling boil over high heat. Remove from the heat and allow to rest for 2 minutes.

2. Combine all ingredients except water in a glass jar or bottle.

3. Add water, put the lid on, and shake vigorously until mixture is fully combined.

4. Store in a sealed container in the refrigerator for up to 1 month.*

*Ketchup may thicken over time. If needed, add a little water to the jar and shake to combine.

SWEET HEAT BBQ SAUCE

Servings:	Prep time:	Cook time:	Wait time:
1.75 cups	7 minutes	15-20 minutes	5 minutes

What You'll Need:

- 6 oz tomato paste
- 1 cup water
- 2-3 tablespoons maple syrup
- 2 teaspoons coco(nut) aminos
- 2 teaspoons apple cider vinegar
- 1 teaspoon lemon juice
- 1 teaspoon chili powder
- ½ teaspoon garlic powder
- ½ teaspoon onion powder
- ½ teaspoon sea salt, or to taste
- ⅛-¼ teaspoon cayenne powder, or to taste
- ¼ teaspoon ground cinnamon
- ¼ teaspoon smoked paprika
- ¼ teaspoon ground cumin

What To Do:

1. Add all ingredients to a small saucepan. Stir to combine.

2. Bring to a rolling boil over medium-high heat. Immediately reduce heat to medium-low, stir, and cover. Allow to simmer for 15 minutes, stirring occasionally.

3. Remove the saucepan from the heat and allow mixture to cool for 5 minutes.

4. Transfer to a jar or bottle with a lid.

5. Store in a sealed container in the refrigerator for up to 1 month.*

*Sauce may thicken over time. If needed, add a little water to the jar and shake to combine.

NOTES

REAL FOOD
Memberships

Through Real Food Memberships, you'll learn the foundations of healthy eating and grow your confidence in the kitchen with access to new recipes, downloadable resources, monthly challenges, and more to keep you motivated on your healthy eating journey.

Learn more and get started today with membership starting at just $5 per month.

Memberships include access to:

✓ The Real Food Recipe Library
✓ The Quality Food Guide
✓ Monthly Challenges
✓ The Full Downloadable Resource Library
✓ The Real Food Test Kitchen
✓ Private Online Community
✓ Monthly Q&A Sessions
✓ Personalized Dietary Recommendations
✓ Monthly Live Group Q&A Call
✓ 1-on-1 Weekly Coaching Calls
✓ Exclusive Deals on Books & Merch

SCAN ME!

Scan the QR code to connect with Real Food Made Simple online!

✓ **Start your Real Food Membership**
✓ **Connect with us on social media**

✓ **Browse the Real Food Merch Shop**
✓ **Apply for our affiliate program**

justrealfoodmadesimple.com